Wok&Stir-Fry

Wok&Stir-Fry

Amazingly tasty...surprisingly simple!

First published in 2010
LOVE FOOD is an imprint of Parragon Books Ltd

Parragon
Queen Street House
4 Queen Street
Bath BA1 1HE, UK

ISBN: 978-1-4075-5387-0

Printed in China

Cover design by Andrew Easton @ Ummagumma
Internal design by Ignition
Additional photography by Charlie Paul (pages 49, 69, 82, 86, 89, 110, 127, 131, 136, 139, 143, 160, 195, 216 & 220)
Additional food styling by Emily Shardlow

Notes for the Reader

• This book uses imperial, metric, and US cup measurements. Follow the same units of measurement throughout; do not mix imperial and metric. All spoon measurements are level: teaspoons are assumed to be 5 ml, and tablespoons are assumed to be 15 ml. Unless otherwise stated, milk is assumed to be whole, eggs and individual vegetables are medium, and pepper is freshly ground black pepper.

• The times given are an approximate guide only. Preparation times differ according to the techniques used by different people and the cooking times may also vary from those given. Optional ingredients, variations, or serving suggestions have not been included in the calculations.

• Recipes using raw or very lightly cooked eggs should be avoided by infants, the elderly, pregnant women, convalescents, and anyone with a chronic illness. Pregnant and breast-feeding women are advised to avoid eating peanuts and peanut products. People with a nut allergy should be aware that some of the prepared ingredients used in the recipes in this book may contain nuts. Always check the package before use.

The workhorse of the Chinese kitchen, the wok has been in use for over 2,000 years. Thanks to its unique shape, the wok can cope with virtually all types of food and cooking techniques. Woks were traditionally made of cast iron, which maintains a steady, even heat. It is worth noting that Chinese cast-iron woks are thinner and lighter than the Western equivalent. They heat up more quickly and also form a more stable layer of seasoning that prevents food from sticking. The downside is that they are prone to shattering if mishandled or dropped. Western cast-iron woks are sturdier but slow to heat up and cool down. Currently, the most commonly used material for woks is carbon steel. Steel woks are relatively lightweight, conduct heat evenly, and are quick to heat up. However, they vary widely in price and quality.

Seasoning a wok
A new steel or iron wok should be scrubbed to remove any rust or factory oil. Place it over medium heat to dry. While still hot, smear all over with a wad of paper towels soaked in cooking oil. Repeat two or three times using clean paper. Let cool, then rinse and dry thoroughly.

Cleaning and maintenance
Wash your wok with hot water but no detergent because this will remove the seasoned coating. Dry over medium heat. Coat with a thin film of oil to prevent rusting.

BASIC TECHNIQUES
Although most often used for stir-frying, the wok can also be used for steaming, boiling, braising, deep-frying, shallow-frying, and smoking if fitted with a lid and a stand.

Stir-frying
Before you begin, have all the ingredients measured and prepared. Cut fresh ingredients into small equal-size pieces so that they cook in the same amount of time. Slicing meat and vegetables diagonally increases the surface area in contact with the hot oil. The wok must be very hot before you add any oil. Use long-handled chopsticks to stir constantly and toss the ingredients so that they all come in contact with the hot oil.

Deep-frying
Use enough oil to give a depth of about 2 inches/ 5 cm. Heat over medium–high heat until a faint haze appears. If the oil is not hot enough, the food will become soggy instead of crisp. Cook in small batches—overcrowding lowers the temperature of the oil and causes uneven cooking. Remove the food with a wire ladle or tongs and drain thoroughly on paper towels.

Braising
Braising is generally used for tougher cuts of meat and vegetables with dense flesh. The ingredients are briefly stir-fried, then simmered in stock until tender.

Steaming
This method is used in China to cook whole fish, dumplings, vegetables, and morsels of poultry and meat. Place the food on a heatproof plate or in a perforated container above boiling liquid in the bottom of a wok. Cover with a lid to trap the steam, which then permeates the food.

DIPPING SAUCES
These traditional dipping sauces are served with many Asian dishes.

Scallion Dipping Sauce
4 tbsp finely chopped scallions
4 tbsp finely chopped fresh ginger
2 tbsp light soy sauce
1 tsp rice vinegar
4 tbsp canola oil

Combine all the ingredients in a bowl and whisk very thoroughly until well blended. For a smooth sauce, process in a blender.

Soy-Ginger Dipping Sauce
3 tbsp soy sauce
2 tsp very finely chopped fresh ginger

Combine the soy sauce and ginger in a small serving bowl. Let stand for 15 minutes for the flavor to deepen.

Sweet, Sour & Spicy Fish Sauce
¾ cup Thai fish sauce
½ cup granulated sugar
¾ cup lime or lemon juice
1 large garlic clove, crushed, sliced, or finely chopped
1–2 fresh red Thai chiles, sliced

Combine the fish sauce and sugar in a small serving bowl and whisk until the sugar is completely dissolved. Stir in the lime juice, garlic, and chiles. Let stand for 20 minutes for the flavor to deepen.

STOCKS

These essential Asian stocks will give your dishes an authentic flavor.

Basic Chinese Stock

Makes about 6 cups

2 lb/900 g chicken portions, such as wings, thighs, and drumsticks, coarsely chopped
2 lb/900 g pork spareribs
1 lb/450 g ham, in one piece
16 cups water
2¾-inch/7-cm piece fresh ginger, unpeeled and thickly sliced
1 celery stalk, coarsely chopped
1 carrot, coarsely chopped
3 large scallions, green parts included, halved lengthwise
2 tsp Chinese rice wine or dry sherry

Put the chicken, pork, and ham in a large pan with enough water to cover. Bring to a boil, then drain in a colander and rinse away the foam under cold running water. Wash out the pan.

Return the meat to the pan with the measured water. Add the ginger, celery, carrot, and scallions, and bring back to a boil, skimming off any foam that forms. Reduce the heat to a very gentle simmer and cook, uncovered, for 2 hours.

Strain the stock through a colander, reserving the liquid and discarding the solids. Pour the liquid through a cheesecloth-lined strainer. Pour back into the pan and add the rice wine. Bring back to a boil, then simmer for 2–3 minutes.

Pour into containers and let cool, then store in the refrigerator. Once thoroughly chilled, remove the solidified fat from the surface.

Spicy Beef Stock

Makes about 6 cups

3 lb 5 oz/1.5 kg beef brisket or boneless shin of beef, cut into large chunks
12 cups water
1 small onion, quartered
2-inch/5-cm piece fresh ginger, unpeeled and thickly sliced
2-inch/5-cm piece cinnamon stick
5 star anise
1 tsp black peppercorns
1 tsp salt

Put the beef in a large pan with enough water to cover. Bring to a boil, then drain in a colander and rinse away the foam under cold running water. Wash out the pan.

Return the meat to the pan with the measured water. Add the onion, ginger, cinnamon stick, star anise, peppercorns, and salt, and bring back to a boil, skimming off any foam that forms. Reduce the heat to a very gentle simmer and cook, uncovered, for 2 hours.

Strain the stock through a colander, reserving the liquid and discarding the solids. Pour the liquid through a cheesecloth-lined strainer.

Pour into containers and let cool, then store in the refrigerator. Once thoroughly chilled, remove the solidified fat from the surface.

Appetizers

SERVES 4

3 strips of lime zest
2 garlic cloves, peeled
2 slices fresh ginger
4 cups chicken stock
1 tbsp peanut or corn oil
6 oz/175 g firm tofu,
   drained and cubed

7 oz/200 g dried fine egg
   noodles
1½ cups sliced shiitake
   mushrooms
1 fresh red chile, seeded
   and sliced
4 scallions, sliced

1 tsp light soy sauce
juice of 1 lime
1 tsp Chinese rice wine
1 tsp sesame oil
chopped fresh cilantro,
   to garnish

Hot & Sour Soup with Tofu

Put the lime zest, garlic, and ginger into a wok with the stock and bring to a boil. Reduce the heat and let simmer for 5 minutes. Remove the lime zest, garlic, and ginger with a slotted spoon and discard.

Meanwhile, heat the peanut oil in a large skillet over high heat, add the tofu, and cook, turning frequently, until golden. Remove the tofu from the skillet and drain on paper towels.

Add the noodles, mushrooms, and chile to the stock and let simmer for 3 minutes. Add the tofu, scallions, soy sauce, lime juice, rice wine, and sesame oil and briefly heat through.

Divide the soup among four individual bowls, sprinkle over the cilantro, and serve immediately.

SERVES 4

4 cups water
2 tsp dashi granules

6 oz/175 g silken tofu, drained and cut into small cubes
4 shiitake mushrooms, finely sliced

4 tbsp miso paste
2 scallions, chopped

Miso Soup

Put the water in a wok with the dashi granules and bring to a boil. Add the tofu and mushrooms, reduce the heat, and let simmer for 3 minutes.

Stir in the miso paste and let simmer gently, stirring, until it has dissolved.

Add the scallions and serve immediately. If you let the soup stand, the miso will settle, so give the soup a thorough stir before serving.

SERVES 6–8

8 cups chicken stock
2 tsp salt
½ tsp white pepper
2 tbsp finely chopped
  scallion
1 tbsp chopped fresh
  cilantro leaves

wontons
6 oz/175 g ground pork,
  not too lean
8 oz/225 g shrimp,
  peeled, deveined, and
  chopped
½ tsp finely chopped
  fresh ginger
1 tbsp light soy sauce
1 tbsp Chinese rice wine

2 tbsp finely chopped
  scallion
pinch of sugar
pinch of white pepper
dash of sesame oil
30 square wonton
  wrappers
1 egg white, lightly
  beaten

Wonton Soup

For the wonton filling, mix together the pork, shrimp, ginger, soy sauce, rice wine, scallion, sugar, pepper, and sesame oil and stir well until the texture is thick and pasty. Set aside for at least 20 minutes.

To make the wontons, place a teaspoon of the filling at the center of a wrapper. Brush the edges with a little egg white. Bring the opposite points toward each other and press the edges together, creating a flowerlike shape. Repeat with the remaining wrappers and filling.

Bring the stock to a boil and add the salt and pepper. Boil the wontons in the stock for about 5 minutes, or until the wrappers begin to wrinkle around the filling.

To serve, divide the scallion among individual bowls, then spoon in the wontons and soup and sprinkle with the cilantro.

SERVES 4

4 cups chicken stock
generous 1 cup fresh or
  frozen corn kernels
1 tbsp sake

½ tsp sugar
1 tbsp cornstarch,
  blended with 2 tbsp
  cold water

1 egg white, lightly
  beaten
2 scallions, thinly sliced,
  plus extra to garnish

Corn Soup

Put the stock in a wok and bring to a boil. Add the corn kernels and cook for
5 minutes, or until tender.

Strain the stock over a bowl, reserving the stock, and transfer the corn to a blender
or food processor. Process to a puree.

Return the stock to the wok. Press the corn puree through a strainer into the wok to
remove any remaining solid pieces.

Bring to a boil, then stir in the sake and sugar. Add the cornstarch mixture and
cook, stirring constantly, until thickened. Drizzle in the beaten egg white, stirring in a
circular motion, then add the scallions.

Ladle the soup into individual bowls, garnish with scallions, and serve immediately.

SERVES 4

4 shallots, chopped
1 large garlic clove, chopped
2 tsp finely chopped fresh ginger
1 tbsp peanut or corn oil
1 lb/450 g sirloin steak, external fat removed, cut into ½-inch/1-cm cubes

5¼ cups Spicy Beef Stock (see page 9)
1 tsp white peppercorns, crushed
5½ oz/150 g dried wide rice noodles
juice of 1 lime
2 tsp Thai fish sauce
½ tsp salt
½ tsp sugar

to garnish/serve
4 scallions, shredded
1 fresh red chile, seeded and cut into thin strips
3 tbsp torn fresh cilantro leaves
lime wedges

Vietnamese Beef & Noodle Soup

Puree the shallots, garlic, and ginger in a food processor or blender, pulsing several times until smooth.

Heat a wok over medium–high heat, then add the oil. Stir-fry the paste for 2 minutes, being careful to avoid letting it burn. Add the beef and stir-fry for 1 minute, until brown, then pour in 4 cups of the stock. Bring to a rapid boil, skimming off any foam that forms. Add the crushed peppercorns, then reduce the heat and gently simmer for 30–35 minutes, or until the meat is tender.

Meanwhile, cook the noodles according to the package directions, until tender.

When the meat is tender, stir in any sticky residue that has formed at the edge of the wok. Add the remaining stock, the lime juice, fish sauce, salt, and sugar. Simmer for a few minutes.

Drain the noodles and divide among individual soup bowls. Ladle the meat and broth over the top. Scatter over the scallions, chile, and cilantro, then serve immediately with lime wedges.

SERVES 6

1 lb/450 g skinless, boneless catfish or cod fillets, cut into large chunks
⅓ cup tamarind concentrate
1⅓ cups fresh pineapple chunks
1 large ripe tomato, peeled, seeded, and cut into 8 wedges

2 fresh red Thai chiles, seeded and thinly sliced into rounds
1 tbsp Thai fish sauce
12 fresh Thai basil leaves, torn
6 fresh saw leaves, torn, or ⅓ cup fresh cilantro leaves
salt and pepper

light fish stock
12 cups water
2 lb 8 oz/1.1 kg fish heads and bones
¾-inch/2-cm piece fresh ginger, thinly sliced
4 scallions, crushed
2–3 tbsp Thai fish sauce

Spicy & Sour Fish & Pineapple Soup

For the stock, put the water and fish heads and bones in a large saucepan and bring to a boil over high heat. Reduce the heat to low–medium, then add the ginger, scallions, and fish sauce and simmer for 1½ hours, or until reduced by about half, skimming off any foam. Strain the stock, discarding the solids, and remove any fat.

Season the fish with salt and pepper to taste. Cover with plastic wrap and chill in the refrigerator for up to 30 minutes.

Pour the stock into a wok and bring to a gentle boil over medium heat. Reduce the heat to low–medium, then add the tamarind concentrate, pineapple, tomato, chiles, and fish sauce and cook for 10 minutes. Add the fish chunks and cook for 5 minutes, or until opaque.

Ladle the soup into individual bowls. Scatter over the torn basil and saw leaves and serve immediately.

SERVES 4

8 oz/225 g dried wide rice noodles

3 cups canned coconut milk

2 fish stock cubes

3 fresh kaffir lime leaves

2 tbsp Thai red curry paste

bunch of scallions, coarsely chopped

2 fresh red chiles, seeded and coarsely chopped

8 oz/225 g squid, cleaned and cut into rings

8 oz/225 g large shrimp, shelled and deveined

handful of fresh cilantro, chopped, plus extra leaves to garnish

Squid & Shrimp Laksa

Soak the noodles in a pan of boiling water for 4 minutes, covered, or cook according to the package directions, until tender. Drain, then rinse under cold running water and set aside.

Put the coconut milk, stock cubes, lime leaves, curry paste, scallions, and chiles in a wok and bring gently to a boil, stirring occasionally. Reduce the heat and simmer, stirring occasionally, for 2–3 minutes, or until the stock cubes and curry paste have dissolved.

Add the squid and shrimp and simmer for 1–2 minutes, or until the squid has plumped up and the shrimp have turned pink. Add the cooked noodles and chopped cilantro and stir well. Ladle into individual bowls and serve immediately, garnished with cilantro leaves.

MAKES 20

6 dried Chinese mushrooms
2 oz/55 g dried fine cellophane noodles
2 tbsp peanut or corn oil, plus extra for deep-frying
1 tbsp finely chopped fresh ginger

generous ⅔ cup julienned carrot
scant 1 cup finely shredded cabbage
1 tbsp finely sliced scallion
1 tbsp light soy sauce
3 oz/85 g tofu, drained and cut into small cubes

½ tsp salt
pinch of white pepper
pinch of sugar
20 egg roll wrappers
1 egg white, lightly beaten
dark soy sauce, to serve

Vegetarian Egg Rolls

Soak the mushrooms in a bowl of warm water for 20 minutes. Squeeze out the excess water from the mushrooms and chop finely, discarding any tough stems.

Cook the noodles according to the package directions, until tender. Drain, rinse under cold running water, and drain again. Chop coarsely and set aside.

Heat a wok over high heat, then add the 2 tablespoons of oil. Toss in the ginger and cook until fragrant. Add the mushrooms and stir-fry for about 2 minutes. Add the carrot, cabbage, and scallion and stir-fry for 1 minute. Add the noodles and light soy sauce and stir-fry for 1 minute. Add the tofu and cook for an additional minute. Season with the salt, pepper, and sugar and mix well. Continue cooking for 1–2 minutes, or until the carrot has softened. Remove from the heat and let the mixture cool.

Place a scant tablespoon of the mixture toward the bottom of an egg roll wrapper. Roll once to secure the filling, then fold in the sides to create a 4 inch/10 cm long egg roll and continue to roll up. Seal with a little of the egg white. Repeat with the remaining wrappers and filling.

Heat enough oil for deep-frying in a wok to 350–375°F/180–190°C, or until a cube of bread browns in 30 seconds. Without overcrowding the pan, cook the rolls for about 5 minutes, or until golden brown and crispy. Serve with dark soy sauce for dipping.

MAKES 20

small pat of butter
1 egg, beaten
4 oz/115 g firm tofu, drained
3 tbsp peanut or corn oil
1 tsp finely chopped garlic
2 oz/55 g lean pork, shredded

4 oz/115 g shrimp, peeled and deveined
½ small carrot, cut into short, thin sticks
4½ oz/125 g canned bamboo shoots, drained and shredded
1 cup finely shredded cabbage

½ cup snow peas, julienned
1 tsp salt
1 tsp light soy sauce
1 tsp Chinese rice wine
pinch of white pepper
20 soft egg roll wrappers
chili bean sauce, to serve

Soft-Wrapped Pork & Shrimp Rolls

Heat the butter in a small heavy-bottom skillet and add the beaten egg. Swirl the egg until it covers the bottom of the skillet. Cook until the egg has set and is cooked through, then turn out onto a plate. Cut the omelet into strips.

Cut the tofu horizontally into thin slices. Heat a wok over medium–high heat, then add 1 tablespoon of the oil. Cook the tofu until it turns golden brown. Cut into thin strips and set aside.

Add the remaining oil to the wok and stir-fry the garlic until fragrant. Add the pork and stir for about 1 minute, then add the shrimp and stir-fry for an additional minute. One by one, stirring well after each, add the carrot, bamboo shoots, cabbage, snow peas, tofu, and, finally, the omelet strips. Season with the salt, soy sauce, rice wine, and pepper. Stir-fry for an additional minute, then turn into a bowl.

Smear an egg roll wrapper with a little chili bean sauce and place a heaped teaspoon of the filling toward the bottom of the wrapper. Roll up the bottom edge to secure the filling, turn in the sides, and continue to roll up gently. Cut each roll diagonally in half and arrange, cut-sides up, on a serving plate. Repeat with the remaining wrappers and filling. Serve immediately with chili bean sauce.

SERVES 4

4 oz/115 g dried fine cellophane noodles
2 lb/900 g mixed vegetables, such as carrots, baby corn, mushrooms, broccoli, snow peas, and onions

6 eggs
4 scallions, diagonally sliced
2½ tbsp peanut or corn oil

3½ oz/100 g canned bamboo shoots, drained
scant 1 cup store-bought sweet-and-sour sauce
salt and pepper

Sweet & Sour Vegetables on Noodle Pancakes

Soak the noodles in enough lukewarm water to cover and let stand for 20 minutes, until softened. Alternatively, cook according to the package directions, until tender. Drain well and use scissors to cut into 3-inch/7.5-cm pieces, then set aside.

Meanwhile, prepare the vegetables as necessary and chop into equal-size chunks.

Beat the eggs in a large bowl, then stir in the noodles and scallions and season to taste with salt and pepper. Heat an 8-inch/20-cm skillet over high heat. Add 1 tablespoon of the oil and swirl it around. Pour in one quarter of the egg mixture and tilt the skillet so it covers the bottom. Reduce the heat to medium and cook for 1 minute, or until the thin pancake is set. Flip it over and continue cooking until the pancake is set. Keep warm while you make three more pancakes.

Heat a wok over high heat. Add the remaining oil and heat until it shimmers. Add the thickest vegetables, such as carrots, first and stir-fry for 30 seconds. Gradually add the remaining vegetables and the bamboo shoots. Stir in the sauce and stir-fry until all the vegetables are tender and the sauce is hot. To serve, spoon the vegetables and sauce over the pancakes and serve.

SERVES 4

5½ oz/150 g tempura mix
4 shiitake mushrooms
4 fresh asparagus spears
4 sweet potato slices

1 red bell pepper, seeded
    and cut into strips
4 onion slices, cut into
    rings
peanut or corn oil, for
    deep-frying

dipping sauce
2 tsp mirin
1 tbsp shoyu (Japanese
    soy sauce)
pinch of dashi granules,
    dissolved in 2 tbsp
    boiling water

Vegetable Tempura

To make the dipping sauce, mix the ingredients together in a small dish.

Mix the tempura with water according to the package directions. Don't try to make the batter smooth—it should be a little lumpy. Drop the vegetables into the batter.

Heat enough oil for deep-frying in a wok to 350–375°F/180–190°C, or until a cube of bread browns in 30 seconds. Lift 2–3 pieces of vegetable out of the batter, carefully drop into the oil, and cook for 2–3 minutes, or until the batter is a light golden color. Remove with a slotted spoon, drain on paper towels, and keep hot while you cook the remaining vegetables.

Serve immediately with the dipping sauce.

SERVES 4

2 large sweet potatoes
2 garlic cloves, crushed
1 small fresh green chile, seeded and chopped
2 fresh cilantro sprigs, chopped
1 tbsp dark soy sauce
all-purpose flour, for dusting

peanut or corn oil, for shallow-frying
sesame seeds, to garnish

soy-tomato sauce
2 tsp vegetable oil
1 garlic clove, finely chopped
1½ tsp finely chopped fresh ginger

3 tomatoes, skinned and chopped
2 tbsp dark soy sauce
1 tbsp lime juice
2 tbsp chopped fresh cilantro

Sweet Potato Cakes with Soy-Tomato Sauce

To make the soy-tomato sauce, heat the oil in a wok and stir-fry the garlic and ginger over medium heat for about 1 minute. Add the tomatoes and stir-fry for an additional 2 minutes. Remove the wok from the heat and stir in the soy sauce, lime juice, and cilantro. Reserve and keep warm.

Peel the sweet potatoes and grate finely. Place the garlic, chile, and cilantro in a mortar and crush to a smooth paste with a pestle. Stir in the soy sauce and mix with the sweet potatoes.

Put some flour on a plate. Divide the mixture into 12 equal portions, toss each portion in the flour until coated, and pat into a flat, round patty shape.

Heat a shallow layer of oil in a skillet. Fry the sweet potato patties, in batches, over high heat until golden, turning once. Drain the sweet potato cakes on paper towels.

Transfer to a serving dish, sprinkle with sesame seeds, and serve immediately with the soy-tomato sauce.

MAKES 24

24 round gyoza wrappers or wonton wrappers
peanut or corn oil, for shallow-frying
2 tbsp Japanese rice vinegar
2 tbsp shoyu (Japanese soy sauce)

filling

scant 1 cup finely shredded Chinese cabbage
2 scallions, finely chopped
6 oz/175 g ground pork
½-inch/1-cm piece fresh ginger, finely grated

2 garlic cloves, crushed
1 tbsp shoyu (Japanese soy sauce)
2 tsp mirin
pinch of white pepper
salt

Pork Gyoza

To make the filling, mix all the filling ingredients together in a bowl. Season to taste with salt.

Lay a gyoza wrapper flat on the palm of your hand and put 1 heaping teaspoon of the filling in the center. Brush a little water around the edges of the wrapper. Fold the sides up to meet in a ridge along the center and press the edges together. Brush the curved edges of the wrapper with a little more water and make a series of little folds along the edges. Repeat with the remaining gyoza wrappers and filling.

Heat a shallow layer of oil in a wok with a lid and add as many gyoza as will fill the bottom of the skillet with just a little space in between. Cook for 2 minutes, or until the undersides are browned.

Add water to a depth of about ⅛ inch/3 mm, cover the wok, and simmer over low heat for 6 minutes, or until the wrappers are translucent and cooked. Uncover and increase the heat to bubble away any excess water. Remove and keep warm while you cook the remaining gyoza.

Put the vinegar in a small dish, stir in the shoyu, and add a splash of water. Serve the gyoza with the sauce for dipping.

MAKES 12-15

12–15 square wonton wrappers
peanut or corn oil, for deep-frying
snipped fresh garlic chives, to garnish
Soy-Ginger Dipping Sauce, to serve (see page 6)

filling
4½ oz/125 g ground, lean sirloin or top round steak
1 scallion, green part included, finely chopped
2 button mushrooms, finely chopped
1 small garlic clove, finely chopped
½ tsp finely chopped fresh ginger
½ tsp soy sauce
¼ tsp salt
¼ tsp white pepper
⅛ tsp Chinese five-spice powder
½ tsp cornstarch
½ egg, beaten

Spicy Beef & Mushroom Wontons

To make the filling, combine the ground steak, scallion, mushrooms, garlic, and ginger in a bowl. Mix the soy sauce, salt, pepper, five-spice powder, and cornstarch to a thin paste. Add the paste to the beef mixture, then stir in the beaten egg. Stir with a fork until well mixed.

Separate the wonton wrappers and place on a tray, rotating them so one corner is facing toward you. Cover with a clean damp dish towel to prevent cracking. Working with one wrapper at a time, place a slightly rounded teaspoon of filling in the bottom corner, ½ inch/1 cm away from the point. Fold the point over the filling, then roll up two thirds of the wrapper, leaving a point at the top. Moisten the right- and left-hand corners with a dab of water. Fold one corner over the other and press lightly to seal. Repeat with the remaining wrappers and filling.

Heat enough oil for deep-frying in a wok to 350–375°F/180–190°C, or until a cube of bread browns in 30 seconds. Deep-fry the wontons in batches for 4–5 minutes, until golden brown and crisp. Remove with a slotted spoon and drain on paper towels. Transfer to a serving platter, garnish with garlic chives, and serve immediately with the dipping sauce.

MAKES 24

24 square wonton wrappers
peanut or corn oil, for deep-frying
fresh garlic chives and lime slices, to garnish

filling
6 oz/175 g white crabmeat, drained if canned and thawed if frozen, flaked
1¾ oz/50 g canned water chestnuts, drained and chopped

1 small fresh red chile, chopped
1 scallion, chopped
1 tbsp cornstarch
1 tsp Chinese rice wine or dry sherry
1 tsp light soy sauce
½ tsp lime juice

Crispy Crab Wontons

To make the filling, mix the crabmeat, water chestnuts, chile, scallion, cornstarch, rice wine, soy sauce, and lime juice in a bowl.

Spread the wonton wrappers out on a work surface and spoon an equal portion of the filling into the center of each wonton wrapper. Dampen the edges of the wonton wrappers with a little water and fold them in half to form triangles. Fold the two bottom corners in toward the center, moisten with a little water to secure, then pinch together to seal.

Heat enough oil for deep-frying in a wok to 350–375°F/180–190°C, or until a cube of bread browns in 30 seconds. Deep-fry the wontons in batches for 2–3 minutes, until golden brown and crisp. Remove with a slotted spoon and drain on paper towels.

Serve the wontons immediately, garnished with garlic chives and lime slices.

MAKES 16

3½ oz/100g shrimp, peeled and deveined
2 egg whites
2 tbsp cornstarch

½ tsp sugar
pinch of salt
2 tbsp finely chopped fresh cilantro

2 slices day-old white bread
peanut or corn oil, for deep-frying

Shrimp Toasts

Pound the shrimp to a paste with a pestle or process briefly in a food processor.

Mix the shrimp with 1 of the egg whites and 1 tablespoon of the cornstarch. Add the sugar and salt and stir in the cilantro. Mix the remaining egg white with the remaining cornstarch.

Remove the crusts from the bread and cut each slice into 8 triangles. Brush the top of each piece with the egg white-and-cornstarch mixture, then add 1 teaspoon of the shrimp mixture. Smooth the top.

Heat enough oil for deep-frying in a wok to 350–375°F/180–190°C, or until a cube of bread browns in 30 seconds. Without overcrowding the wok, cook the toasts, shrimp-side up, for about 2 minutes. Turn and cook for an additional 2 minutes, or until beginning to turn golden brown. Remove with a slotted spoon, drain on paper towels, and serve warm.

SERVES 4

8 chicken wings, each wing chopped into 3 pieces
5 tbsp peanut or corn oil
6 tbsp Basic Chinese Stock (see page 9)
2 tbsp chopped fresh cilantro

marinade
1½ tbsp Chinese rice wine or dry sherry
1 tbsp soy sauce
1 tbsp rice vinegar
1½ tbsp sugar
¾ tsp salt
⅛ tsp Chinese five-spice powder
3 tbsp hoisin sauce
1 tsp finely chopped fresh ginger

Glazed Chicken Wings

To make the marinade, combine the rice wine, soy sauce, and vinegar in a small bowl. Add the sugar, salt, and five-spice powder and stir until dissolved. Mix in the hoisin sauce and ginger.

Put the chopped chicken wings in a shallow dish and pour in the marinade, turning to coat. Let marinate for 1 hour at room temperature, or overnight in the refrigerator.

Heat a wok over high heat, add the oil, and, when it is almost smoking, add the chicken wings and marinade. Stir-fry for 5 minutes, then sprinkle with 4 tablespoons of the stock and stir-fry for an additional 4 minutes.

Using tongs, transfer the chicken wings to a serving dish and sprinkle with the cilantro. Pour off and discard most of the oil from the wok and return to the heat. Add the remaining stock and stir with a wooden spoon until blended, scraping up the sticky sediment. Pour into a small bowl and serve with the chicken wings as a dipping sauce.

MAKES 36

- 1 lb/450 g ground lamb
- 1 garlic clove, finely chopped
- 1 tsp finely chopped fresh ginger
- 1½ tbsp soy sauce
- 1 tsp Chinese rice wine or dry sherry
- ½ tsp salt
- ½ tsp sugar
- ½ tsp white pepper
- ½ tbsp cornstarch
- 1 egg, beaten
- peanut or corn oil, for shallow-frying
- shredded Chinese cabbage and snipped fresh garlic chives, to garnish
- Scallion Dipping Sauce, to serve (see page 6)

Fried Lamb Balls with Scallion Sauce

Combine the lamb, garlic, and ginger in a bowl. Mix the soy sauce, rice wine, salt, sugar, pepper, and cornstarch to a thin paste. Add the paste to the lamb mixture, then stir in the beaten egg. Stir with a fork until well mixed. Pinch off small pieces of the mixture and roll between your palms to form balls the size of large marbles.

Heat a wok over high heat, add a shallow layer of oil, and, when it is almost smoking, add the balls. Fry the balls in batches for 3 minutes, turning halfway through. Drain on paper towels.

Arrange a bed of shredded Chinese cabbage on a serving platter. Arrange the lamb balls on top and sprinkle with garlic chives. Serve immediately with the dipping sauce.

SERVES 4

1 iceberg lettuce
1 tbsp peanut or corn oil
1 onion, finely chopped
1 fresh red chile, seeded
 and chopped
12 oz/350 g ground pork

7 oz/200 g canned water
 chestnuts, drained and
 chopped
3–4 tbsp Thai soy sauce
1 tsp jaggery or light
 brown sugar

1–2 tbsp Thai green curry
 paste
2 tbsp chopped fresh
 cilantro, plus extra to
 garnish
lime wedges, to serve

Lettuce Wraps

Separate the lettuce leaves, wash well in cold water, and shake dry. Place all the leaves upside down on a large plate and let chill in the refrigerator for 2 hours.

Heat a wok over medium–high heat, then add the oil. Stir-fry the onion and chile for 30 seconds. Add the pork and stir-fry for 8–10 minutes, until browned and crisp. Stir in the water chestnuts, soy sauce, jaggery, curry paste, and cilantro, and cook for an additional 2–3 minutes.

Spoon the pork mixture into the chilled lettuce leaves and transfer to a serving plate. Scatter over the cilantro and serve immediately with lime wedges.

SERVES 4

8 baby carrots, scraped and halved lengthwise

1⅔ cups broccoli florets

1 large head of bok choy

1 tbsp peanut or corn oil

1 red onion, sliced

1–2 fresh Thai chiles, seeded and sliced

1-inch/2.5-cm piece fresh ginger, grated

2 whole star anise

1 red bell pepper, seeded and cut into strips

1 orange bell pepper, seeded and cut into strips

8 baby zucchini, diagonally sliced

8 baby corn, halved lengthwise

2 tbsp orange juice

1 tbsp soy sauce

1 tbsp cashew nuts

Warm Asian-Style Salad

Bring a small pan of water to a boil and add the halved carrots. Cook for 3 minutes, then add the broccoli and cook for an additional 2 minutes. Drain and plunge into cold water, then drain again and set aside.

Arrange 2 of the bok choy leaves on a large serving platter. Shred the remainder and set aside.

Heat a wok over medium–high heat, then add the oil. Add the onion, chiles, ginger, and star anise and stir-fry for 1 minute. Add the bell peppers, zucchini, and baby corn and stir-fry for an additional 2 minutes.

Pour in the orange juice and soy sauce and continue to stir-fry for 1 minute before adding the reserved shredded bok choy. Stir-fry for 2 minutes, or until the vegetables are tender but still firm to the bite. Arrange the warm salad on the prepared serving platter, scatter the cashew nuts over the top, and serve immediately.

SERVES 4

8 outer leaves of romaine lettuce or similar dark, crisp lettuce leaves
3½ oz/100 g green beans, lightly cooked
8 baby carrots, lightly cooked
6 new potatoes, cooked until just tender

1 tbsp peanut or corn oil
generous ¾ cup fresh bean sprouts
3¼-inch/8-cm piece cucumber, seeded and cut into 1½-inch/4-cm batons
4 eggs, hard-cooked
1 small mild onion, sliced into rings

sauce
4 tbsp canned coconut milk
3 tbsp smooth peanut butter
juice of ½ lime
2 tsp light soy sauce
dash of Tabasco sauce or any chili sauce

Gado Gado

Tear the lettuce leaves, if large, and arrange on four individual serving plates or a large serving platter. Halve the beans and cut the carrots, as necessary, into batons. Cut the potatoes into chunks if large, then arrange on the plates or platter with the beans and carrots.

Heat a wok over high heat, then add the oil. Add the bean sprouts and stir-fry for 2 minutes, or until lightly cooked and still crisp. Remove with a slotted spoon and sprinkle over the cooked vegetables with the cucumber. Peel and quarter the eggs, then arrange on top of the salad.

Add the onion rings to the oil remaining in the wok and stir-fry over high heat for 5 minutes, or until golden and crisp. Combine all the ingredients for the sauce in a small bowl and pour over the salad. Top with the onion rings and serve immediately.

SERVES 4

4 boneless chicken breasts
2 tbsp Thai red curry paste
2 tbsp peanut or corn oil

1 head of Chinese cabbage, shredded
1 cup bok choy, torn into large pieces
½ head of savoy cabbage, shredded

2 shallots, finely chopped
2 garlic cloves, crushed
1 tbsp rice vinegar
2 tbsp sweet chili sauce
2 tbsp Thai soy sauce

Red Chicken Salad

Score the chicken several times and rub the curry paste into each cut. Cover and let chill overnight.

Cook the chicken in a wok over medium heat for 5–6 minutes, turning once or twice, until cooked through. Keep warm.

Wipe out the wok with paper towels. Heat 1 tablespoon of the oil in the wok and stir-fry the Chinese cabbage, bok choy, and savoy cabbage until just wilted. Add the remaining oil, shallots, and garlic and stir-fry until just tender but not browned. Add the vinegar, chili sauce, and soy sauce. Remove from the heat.

Arrange the stir-fried leaves on four individual serving plates. Slice the chicken, arrange on top, and drizzle the hot sauce over the dish. Serve immediately.

SERVES 3

7 oz/200 g dried wide rice noodles
2 carrots
2 celery stalks
1 cucumber
3 duck breasts, about 5 oz/140 g each

peanut sauce
2 garlic cloves, crushed
2 tbsp dark brown sugar
2 tbsp peanut butter
2 tbsp coconut cream
2 tbsp soy sauce
2 tbsp rice vinegar
2 tbsp sesame oil
½ tsp black pepper
½ tsp Chinese five-spice powder
½ tsp ground ginger

Asian Duck & Noodle Salad with Peanut Sauce

Cook the noodles according to the package directions, until tender. Drain, rinse under cold water, and set aside.

Preheat the broiler. Cut the carrots, celery, and cucumber into thin strips and set aside.

Broil the duck breasts under the preheated broiler for about 5 minutes on each side, until cooked through. Let cool.

Meanwhile, heat all the ingredients for the sauce in a small pan until combined and the sugar has dissolved completely. Stir until smooth.

Slice the duck breasts. Divide the noodles among three individual serving plates. Scatter the reserved carrots, celery, and cucumber over the noodles, arrange the duck slices on top, and drizzle with the sauce. Serve immediately.

SERVES 4

4 cups chicken stock
scant 1 cup mixed long-
 grain and wild rice
2 tbsp peanut or corn oil
8 oz/225 g skinless,
 boneless turkey breast,
 trimmed of all visible fat
 and cut into thin strips

2 cups snow peas
4 oz/115 g oyster
 mushrooms, torn into
 pieces
¼ cup shelled pistachios,
 finely chopped
2 tbsp chopped fresh
 cilantro

1 tbsp snipped fresh
 garlic chives, plus extra
 to garnish
1 tbsp black rice vinegar
salt and pepper

Turkey + Rice Salad

Set aside 3 tablespoons of the stock and bring the remainder to a boil in a large pan. Add the rice and cook for 30 minutes, or until tender. Drain and let cool slightly.

Meanwhile, heat a wok over medium heat, then add 1 tablespoon of the oil. Stir-fry the turkey for 3–4 minutes, or until cooked through. Using a slotted spoon, transfer the turkey to a dish. Add the snow peas and mushrooms to the wok and stir-fry for 1 minute. Add the reserved stock, bring to a boil, then reduce the heat, cover, and let simmer for 3–4 minutes. Transfer the vegetables to the dish and let cool slightly.

Mix together the rice, turkey, snow peas, mushrooms, pistachios, cilantro, and garlic chives, then season to taste with salt and pepper. Drizzle with the remaining oil and the vinegar and garnish with garlic chives. Serve warm.

SERVES 4

1 tbsp peanut or corn oil
1 fresh serrano chile, seeded and finely chopped
scant 1 cup snow peas, halved diagonally
6 scallions, finely shredded

2 heaping tbsp corn kernels, thawed if frozen
5½ oz/150 g white crabmeat, drained if canned
2 oz/55 g shrimp, peeled and deveined
1 carrot, grated

¾ cup fresh bean sprouts
5 cups baby spinach leaves
1 tbsp finely grated orange rind
2 tbsp orange juice
1 tbsp chopped fresh cilantro

Spicy Warm Crab & Shrimp Salad

Heat a wok over medium heat, then add the oil. Add the chile and snow peas, then stir-fry for 2 minutes.

Add the scallions and corn and continue to stir-fry for an additional minute.

Add the crabmeat, shrimp, carrot, bean sprouts, and spinach. Stir in the orange rind and juice and stir-fry for 2–3 minutes, or until the spinach has begun to wilt and everything is cooked. Divide among four serving bowls, sprinkle with the cilantro, and serve immediately.

Meat & Poultry

SERVES 4

10 oz/280 g beef tenderloin, cut into slivers
8 oz/225 g dried medium egg noodles
2 tbsp peanut or corn oil
1 onion, finely sliced
1 green bell pepper, finely sliced

1 cup fresh bean sprouts
1 tsp salt
pinch of sugar
2 tsp Chinese rice wine
2 tbsp light soy sauce
1 tbsp dark soy sauce
1 tbsp finely shredded scallion

marinade
1 tsp light soy sauce
dash of sesame oil
½ tsp Chinese rice wine
pinch of white pepper

Beef Chow Mein

Combine all the marinade ingredients in a bowl and marinate the beef for at least 20 minutes.

Cook the noodles in a pan of boiling water for 4–5 minutes, or according to the package directions, until tender. Drain, rinse under cold water, and set aside.

Heat a wok over high heat, then add the oil. Stir-fry the beef for about 1 minute, or until it has changed color. Stir in the onion and cook for 1 minute, then add the bell pepper and bean sprouts. Cook until any water from the vegetables has evaporated.

Add the salt, sugar, rice wine, and soy sauces. Stir in the noodles and toss for 1 minute. Finally, stir in the scallion and serve.

SERVES 4

1 lb 2 oz/500 g beef tenderloin, cut into thin strips
1½ tbsp sesame seeds
½ cup beef stock
2 tbsp soy sauce
2 tbsp grated fresh ginger

2 garlic cloves, finely chopped
1 tsp cornstarch
½ tsp chile flakes
3 tbsp peanut or corn oil
1 large head of broccoli, cut into florets

1 yellow bell pepper, seeded and thinly sliced
1 fresh red chile, seeded and finely sliced
1 tbsp chili oil, to taste
1 tbsp chopped fresh cilantro, to garnish

Hot Sesame Beef

Mix the beef strips with 1 tablespoon of the sesame seeds in a small bowl. In a separate bowl, whisk together the stock, soy sauce, ginger, garlic, cornstarch, and chile flakes.

Heat a wok with a lid over medium–high heat, then add 1 tablespoon of the peanut oil. Stir-fry the beef strips for 2–3 minutes. Remove and set aside.

Discard any oil remaining in the wok, then wipe with paper towels to remove any stray sesame seeds. Heat the remaining peanut oil and add the broccoli, bell pepper, chile, and chili oil, then stir-fry for 2–3 minutes. Stir in the stock mixture, then cover and simmer for 2 minutes.

Return the beef to the wok and simmer, stirring occasionally, until the juices thicken. Cook for an additional 1–2 minutes.

Transfer to serving plates and sprinkle over the remaining sesame seeds and the cilantro. Serve immediately.

SERVES 4

1 tbsp peanut or corn oil
1 large dried chile,
   seeded and snipped
   into 3 pieces
½ tsp Sichuan pepper
3½ oz/100 g ground beef
2 tsp light soy sauce
10½ oz/300 g dried fine
   rice noodles

1 tbsp chopped roasted
   peanuts
1 tbsp chopped fresh
   cilantro

sauce
1 tbsp preserved
   vegetables
½ tsp lightly roasted
   and crushed Sichuan
   pepper

scant ½ cup chicken
   stock
1 tsp black rice vinegar
1 tsp chili oil
1 tsp dark soy sauce
1 tbsp light soy sauce
1 tbsp sesame paste
a few drops of sesame oil
2 scallions, finely
   chopped

Dan Dan Noodles

Heat a wok over medium-high heat, then add the peanut oil. Toss in the chile and Sichuan pepper, then add the meat and stir rapidly. When the meat has changed color, add the light soy sauce and continue to cook until the meat is well browned.

Carefully mix the sauce ingredients together and pour into four individual serving dishes.

Cook the noodles according to the package directions, until tender. When cooked, drain and divide among the serving dishes.

Top with the meat mixture, then sprinkle with the peanuts and cilantro. Serve immediately.

SERVES 2–3

1½ tbsp Sichuan pepper
½ tsp salt
12 oz/350 g porterhouse steak or top round steak
7 oz/200 g mixed small mushrooms, such as cremini, enoki, and buna shimeji

½ tbsp cornstarch
½ cup Spicy Beef Stock (see page 9) or beef stock
2 tsp Chinese rice wine or dry sherry
4 tsp soy sauce
3 tbsp peanut or corn oil
1 shallot, finely chopped

1 tsp finely chopped fresh ginger
1 large garlic clove, thinly sliced
3 tbsp chopped fresh cilantro

Beef with Mixed Mushrooms

Place the Sichuan pepper in a mortar with the salt and grind with a pestle. Sprinkle over both sides of the meat, pressing in well. Slice the meat diagonally across the grain into thin, bite-size pieces and set aside.

Wipe the mushrooms with damp paper towels. If using clumping mushrooms, such as enoki and buna shimeji, slice off the root and separate the clump. Slice any large mushrooms in half.

Mix the cornstarch to a paste with 2 tablespoons of the stock. Add the rice wine and soy sauce, mixing well.

Heat a wok over medium–high heat, then add 1 tablespoon of the oil. Fry the shallot and ginger for 1 minute. Add the garlic and fry for a few seconds, then add the mushrooms and 2 tablespoons of the remaining stock. Stir-fry for 4 minutes. Add the cornstarch mixture and the remaining stock. Bring to a boil, stirring, then reduce the heat and simmer for 2 minutes. Transfer to a warmed serving dish.

Wipe out the wok with paper towels, then heat over high heat. Add the remaining oil. Add the beef and stir-fry for 3 minutes. Add to the mushroom mixture and sprinkle with the cilantro. Serve immediately.

SERVES 4

2 tbsp peanut or corn oil
8 oz/225 g shallots, coarsely chopped
1 garlic clove, crushed
1 lb/450 g beef tenderloin, cut into 1-inch/2.5-cm cubes

2 tbsp Masaman curry paste
3 potatoes, cut into 1-inch/2.5-cm cubes
1¾ cups canned coconut milk
2 tbsp soy sauce

⅔ cup beef stock
1 tsp jaggery or light brown sugar
½ cup unsalted peanuts
handful of fresh cilantro, chopped
cooked noodles, to serve

Masaman Curry

Heat a wok over medium–high heat, then add the oil. Add the shallots and garlic and stir-fry for 1–2 minutes, or until softened. Add the beef and curry paste and stir-fry over high heat for 2–3 minutes, or until browned all over.

Add the potatoes, coconut milk, soy sauce, stock, and jaggery and bring gently to a boil, stirring occasionally. Reduce the heat and simmer for 8–10 minutes, or until the potatoes are tender.

Meanwhile, heat a separate dry skillet until hot, then add the peanuts and cook over medium–high heat, shaking the skillet frequently, for 2–3 minutes, or until lightly browned. Add to the curry with the cilantro and stir well. Serve immediately with noodles.

SERVES 4

1 lb 2 oz/500 g beef tenderloin, cut into thin strips
peanut or vegetable oil, for deep-frying
3 celery stalks, cut into thin strips

1 red bell pepper, seeded and cut into thin strips
1 fresh red chile, seeded and finely sliced
lime wedges and Sweet, Sour & Spicy Fish Sauce (see page 6), to serve

marinade
1 tsp salt
2 tbsp Thai fish sauce

Thai Marinated Beef with Celery

To make the marinade, mix the salt and fish sauce in a large bowl and set aside. Add the beef and toss to coat. Cover with plastic wrap and put in the refrigerator for 1 hour to marinate.

Heat enough oil for deep-frying in a wok to 180–190°C/350–375°F, or until a cube of bread browns in 30 seconds. Deep-fry the beef in batches for 2–3 minutes, until crispy. Remove the wok from the heat and, using a slotted spoon, lift out the meat and drain it on paper towels. Drain all but 2 tablespoons of the oil from the wok.

Reheat the remaining oil in the wok and stir-fry the celery, bell pepper, and chile for 1 minute. Add the beef and cook for 2–3 minutes.

Serve immediately with lime wedges and Sweet, Sour, and Spicy Fish Sauce.

SERVES 4

peanut or corn oil, for deep-frying
8 oz/225 g pork tenderloin, cut into ½-inch/1-cm cubes
1 onion, sliced
1 green bell pepper, seeded and sliced
1⅓ cups pineapple chunks
1 small carrot, cut into thin strips

1 oz/25 g canned bamboo shoots, drained and halved
cooked rice, to serve

batter
scant ¾ cup all-purpose flour
1 tbsp cornstarch
1½ tsp baking powder
1 tbsp peanut or corn oil

sauce
⅔ cup light brown sugar
2 tbsp cornstarch
½ cup rice vinegar
2 garlic cloves, crushed
4 tbsp tomato paste
6 tbsp pineapple juice

Sweet & Sour Pork

To make the batter, sift the all-purpose flour into a mixing bowl with the cornstarch and baking powder. Add the oil and stir in enough water to make a thick, smooth batter (about ¾ cup).

Heat enough oil for deep-frying in a wok to 350–375°F/180–190°C, or until a cube of bread browns in 30 seconds. Dip the cubes of pork into the batter and deep-fry in batches until the pork is cooked through. Remove the pork from the wok with a slotted spoon and drain on paper towels. Set aside and keep the pork pieces warm until they are required.

Drain all but 1 tablespoon of oil from the wok and return it to the heat. Add the onion, bell pepper, pineapple, carrot, and bamboo shoots and cook for 1–2 minutes. Remove from the wok with a slotted spoon and set aside.

Mix all of the sauce ingredients together and pour into the wok. Bring to a boil, stirring until thickened and clear. Cook for 1 minute, then return the pork and vegetables to the wok. Cook for an additional 1–2 minutes, then transfer to individual dishes and serve immediately with rice.

SERVES 4

1 lb 2 oz/500 g pork tenderloin, cubed
2 tbsp cornstarch
3 tbsp soy sauce
1 tbsp rice vinegar
1 cup water
2 tbsp peanut or corn oil
2 leeks, sliced thinly

1 red bell pepper, seeded and cut into thin strips
1 zucchini, cut into thin strips
1 carrot, cut into thin strips
pinch of salt
cooked wild rice, to serve

marinade
1 tbsp soy sauce
pinch of chile flakes

Sichuan-Style Pork Stir-Fry

To make the marinade, mix the soy sauce and chile flakes in a bowl. Add the pork and toss to coat. Cover with plastic wrap and let stand for 30 minutes. Combine the cornstarch, soy sauce, and vinegar in a small bowl. Stir in the water gradually, then set aside.

Heat a wok over medium–high heat, then add 1 tablespoon of the oil. Add the pork and marinade mixture and stir-fry for 2–3 minutes. Remove the pork from the wok with a slotted spoon and set aside.

Heat the remaining oil in the wok, then add the leeks and bell pepper and stir-fry for 2 minutes. Add the zucchini, carrot, and salt and stir-fry for an additional 2 minutes.

Stir in the pork and the cornstarch mixture and bring to a boil, stirring constantly, until the sauce thickens. Remove from the heat.

Serve immediately with wild rice.

SERVES 4

12 oz/350 g pork tenderloin, cubed
2 tbsp peanut or corn oil
5 cups sliced mushrooms
1 zucchini, thinly sliced
2 carrots, thinly sliced

4 oz/115 g canned bamboo shoots, drained
4 oz/115 g canned water chestnuts, drained and thinly sliced
1 garlic clove, crushed
½ cup chicken stock
cooked rice, to serve

marinade
1 lemongrass stalk, finely sliced
2 tbsp Thai fish sauce
4 tbsp shredded fresh basil
juice of 1 lime

Pork with Basil + Lemongrass

To make the marinade, mix the lemongrass, fish sauce, basil, and lime juice in a bowl. Stir in the pork and toss well to coat. Cover with plastic wrap and chill in the refrigerator for 1–2 hours.

Heat a wok over medium heat, then add 1 tablespoon of the oil. Add the meat and the marinade and stir-fry until the pork is browned. Remove from the wok, set aside, and keep warm.

Add the remaining oil to the wok and heat. Add all the vegetables and the garlic and stir-fry for about 3 minutes.

Return the pork to the wok and add the stock. Cook for 5 minutes, or until the stock is reduced.

Transfer to individual serving dishes and serve immediately with rice.

SERVES 4

8 oz/225 g dried wide
  rice noodles
2 tbsp peanut or corn oil
4 scallions, coarsely
  chopped
2 garlic cloves, crushed
2 fresh red chiles, seeded
  and sliced

8 oz/225 g pork
  tenderloin, trimmed
  and thinly sliced
4 oz/115 g large cooked
  peeled shrimp
juice of 1 lime
2 tbsp Thai fish sauce
2 eggs, beaten

$\frac{1}{3}$ cup fresh bean sprouts
handful of fresh cilantro,
  chopped
$\frac{1}{3}$ cup chopped unsalted
  peanuts
lime wedges, to serve

Pad Thai

Soak the noodles in a large pan of boiling water, covered, for 10 minutes, or cook according to the package directions, until tender. Drain, then rinse under cold running water and set aside.

Heat a wok over high heat, then add the oil. Add the scallions, garlic, and chiles and stir-fry for 1–2 minutes. Add the pork and stir-fry for 1–2 minutes, or until browned all over.

Add the shrimp, lime juice, fish sauce, and eggs and stir-fry over medium heat for 2–3 minutes, or until the eggs have set and the shrimp are heated through.

Add the bean sprouts, most of the cilantro, the peanuts, and the noodles and stir-fry for 30 seconds, or until heated through. Transfer to serving plates, sprinkle over the remaining cilantro, and serve immediately with lime wedges.

SERVES 4

1 lb/450 g lean boneless lamb (leg or loin fillet)
2 tbsp peanut or corn oil
2 garlic cloves, crushed
4 shallots, chopped
2 lemongrass stalks, sliced

6 fresh kaffir lime leaves
1 tbsp tamarind paste
2 tbsp jaggery or light brown sugar
2 fresh red Thai chiles, seeded and finely chopped

2½ cups canned coconut milk
10 cherry tomatoes, halved
1 tbsp chopped fresh cilantro, plus extra to garnish
cooked rice, to serve

Lamb with Lime Leaves

Using a sharp knife, cut the lamb into thin strips or cubes. Set aside until required.

Heat a wok over high heat, then add the oil. Add the garlic, shallots, lemongrass, lime leaves, tamarind paste, jaggery, and chiles to the wok and stir-fry for 2 minutes.

Add the lamb to the wok and stir-fry for 5 minutes, tossing well so that the lamb is evenly coated in the spice mixture.

Pour the coconut milk into the wok and bring to a boil. Reduce the heat and let simmer for 20 minutes.

Add the cherry tomatoes and chopped cilantro to the wok and simmer for 5 minutes. Transfer to individual serving dishes, sprinkle with cilantro, and serve immediately with rice.

SERVES 4

4 tbsp peanut or corn oil
1 lb 4 oz/550 g lamb leg steaks, thinly sliced
1 large onion, finely chopped
2 garlic cloves, finely chopped

2 fresh red chiles, seeded and thinly sliced
1½ cups snow peas
7¾ cups spinach leaves, coarse stalks removed
2 tbsp lime juice

3 tbsp oyster sauce
2 tbsp Thai fish sauce
2 tsp superfine sugar
5 tbsp chopped fresh mint
salt and pepper

Stir-Fried Lamb with Snow Peas & Spinach

Heat a wok over high heat, then add the oil. Add the lamb and stir-fry for 2–3 minutes, or until browned all over. Remove with a slotted spoon and drain on paper towels.

Add the onion, garlic, and chiles to the wok and stir-fry for 3 minutes. Add the snow peas and stir-fry for 2 minutes, then stir in the spinach and return the lamb to the wok.

Add the lime juice, oyster sauce, fish sauce, and sugar and cook, stirring constantly, for 4 minutes, or until the lamb is cooked through and tender. Stir in the mint, season to taste with salt and pepper, and serve immediately.

SERVES 4–6

4 tsp soy sauce
1 tbsp cornstarch
1 tbsp Chinese rice wine or dry sherry
¼ tsp salt
12 oz/350 g skinless, boneless chicken breasts, cut into cubes
6 tbsp Basic Chinese Stock (see page 9) or chicken stock

1 tbsp oyster sauce
4 tbsp peanut or corn oil
1 tsp finely chopped fresh ginger
1 large garlic clove, thinly sliced
4 scallions, white and green parts separated, diagonally sliced into ¾-inch/2-cm pieces
½ tbsp crushed white peppercorns

8 baby corn, halved diagonally
½ small red bell pepper, seeded and thinly sliced
8 oz/225 g canned water chestnuts, drained
scant 1 cup snow peas, halved diagonally

Peppered Chicken Stir-Fry

In a small bowl, combine half of the soy sauce, the cornstarch, rice wine, and salt. Put the chicken pieces in a shallow dish and pour over the soy sauce mixture, stirring to coat. Let stand for 15 minutes.

Mix the remaining soy sauce with the stock and oyster sauce and set aside.

Heat a wok over high heat, then add the oil. Add the chicken and stir-fry for 3 minutes, until no longer pink. Remove from the wok with a slotted spoon and drain on paper towels.

Reduce the heat slightly, then add the ginger, garlic, white scallion, and crushed peppercorns and stir for a few seconds. Add the baby corn, bell pepper, and water chestnuts. Stir-fry for 2 minutes, then return the chicken to the wok. Add the snow peas and the soy sauce mixture and stir-fry for 1–2 minutes, until the sauce is thickened.

Sprinkle with the green scallion and cook for a few more seconds. Serve immediately.

SERVES 4

2 tbsp peanut or corn oil
1 garlic clove, chopped
3 scallions, sliced
4 skinless, boneless
  chicken breasts, cut
  into bite-size chunks

1 tbsp grated fresh ginger
½ tsp chili powder
1⅓ cups snow peas
8 baby corn

2 tbsp smooth peanut
  butter
1 tbsp light soy sauce
cooked rice, to serve

Chicken & Peanut Stir-Fry

Heat a wok over medium–high heat, then add the oil. Add the garlic and scallions and stir-fry for 1 minute. Add the chicken, ginger, and chili powder and stir-fry for 4 minutes. Add the snow peas and baby corn and cook for 2 minutes.

In a bowl, mix together the peanut butter and soy sauce, then add it to the wok. Stir-fry for an additional minute.

Remove from the heat, transfer to individual serving dishes, and serve with rice.

SERVES 4

2 tbsp peanut or corn oil
4 scallions, coarsely
   chopped
2 tbsp Thai green curry
   paste
3 cups canned coconut
   milk

1 chicken stock cube
6 skinless, boneless
   chicken breasts, about
   4 oz/115 g each, cut
   into 1-inch/2.5-cm
   cubes

large handful of fresh
   cilantro, chopped
1 tsp salt
cooked rice, to serve

Thai Green Chicken Curry

Heat a wok over medium–high heat, then add the oil. Add the scallions and stir-fry for 30 seconds, or until starting to soften.

Add the curry paste, coconut milk, and stock cube and bring gently to a boil, stirring occasionally. Add the chicken, half the cilantro, and the salt and stir well. Reduce the heat and simmer gently for 8–10 minutes, or until the chicken is cooked through and tender. Stir in the remaining cilantro. Serve immediately with rice.

SERVES 4

¼ cup chicken stock
2 tbsp soy sauce
2 tbsp Chinese rice wine
  or dry sherry
3 tsp cornstarch
1 egg white, beaten
½ tsp salt
4 tbsp peanut or corn oil

1 lb/450 g skinless,
  boneless chicken
  breast, cut into strips
5 cups sliced mushrooms
1 head of broccoli, cut
  into florets
1¼ cups fresh bean
  sprouts

3½ oz/100 g canned
  water chestnuts,
  drained and thinly
  sliced
generous 1 cup
  pistachios
cooked rice, to serve

Chicken with Pistachios

Combine the stock, soy sauce, and rice wine with 1 teaspoon of the cornstarch. Stir well and set aside.

Combine the egg white, salt, 2 tablespoons of the oil, and the remaining cornstarch. Toss the chicken in the mixture to coat.

Heat a wok over high heat, then add the remaining oil. Add the chicken in batches and stir-fry until golden. Remove from the wok and drain on paper towels, then set aside and keep warm.

Add the mushrooms and broccoli to the wok and cook for 2–3 minutes.

Return the chicken to the wok and add the bean sprouts, water chestnuts, and pistachios. Stir-fry until all the ingredients are warmed through. Add the stock mixture and cook, stirring continuously, until thickened.

Serve immediately with rice.

SERVES 4

1 tbsp peanut or corn oil
1 garlic clove, finely
  chopped
1-inch/2.5-cm piece fresh
  ginger, finely chopped
1 small fresh red chile,
  seeded and finely
  chopped
12 oz/350 g skinless,
  boneless chicken
  breasts, cut into thin
  strips

1 tbsp Thai seven-spice
  powder
1 red bell pepper, seeded
  and sliced
1 yellow bell pepper,
  seeded and sliced
2 zucchini, thinly sliced
8 oz/225 g canned
  bamboo shoots,
  drained

2 tbsp Chinese rice wine
  or dry sherry
1 tbsp light soy sauce
2 tbsp chopped fresh
  cilantro, plus extra
  leaves to garnish
salt and pepper

Thai-Spiced Chicken with Zucchini

Heat a wok over high heat, then add the oil. Add the garlic, ginger, and chile and stir-fry for 30 seconds to release the flavors. Add the chicken and Thai seasoning and stir-fry for 4 minutes, until the chicken has colored all over.

Add the bell peppers and zucchini and stir-fry for 1–2 minutes, until slightly softened. Stir in the bamboo shoots and stir-fry for an additional 2–3 minutes, until the chicken is cooked through and tender.

Add the rice wine, soy sauce, and salt and pepper to taste and sizzle for 1–2 minutes. Stir in the chopped cilantro and serve immediately, garnished with cilantro leaves.

SERVES 4

2 boneless chicken breasts, with or without skin, cut into ½-inch/1-cm cubes
1 tbsp peanut or corn oil
10 dried red chiles, or to taste, snipped into 2–3 pieces
1 tsp Sichuan pepper
3 garlic cloves, finely sliced
1-inch/2.5-cm piece fresh ginger, finely sliced
1 tbsp coarsely chopped scallion, white part only
generous ½ cup roasted peanuts
cooked rice, to serve

marinade
2 tsp light soy sauce
1 tsp Chinese rice wine
½ tsp sugar

sauce
1 tsp light soy sauce
1 tsp dark soy sauce
1 tsp black Chinese rice vinegar
a few drops of sesame oil
2 tbsp chicken stock
1 tsp sugar

Gong Bau Chicken

Combine all the marinade ingredients in a bowl. Add the chicken, toss well, and let marinate, covered, for at least 20 minutes. Combine all the sauce ingredients in a separate bowl and set aside.

Heat a wok over high heat, then add the peanut oil. Stir-fry the chiles and Sichuan pepper until crisp and fragrant. Toss in the chicken pieces. When they begin to color, add the garlic, ginger, and scallion. Stir-fry for about 5 minutes, or until the chicken is cooked.

Pour in the sauce, mix together thoroughly, then stir in the peanuts. Serve immediately with rice.

SERVES 4

small pat of butter
2 large eggs, beaten
½ tbsp peanut or corn oil
6 shallots, quartered
3¼ cups diced cooked
  chicken

3 tbsp light soy sauce
2 carrots, diced
1 celery stalk, diced
1 red bell pepper, seeded
  and diced
1½ cups fresh peas

½ cup fresh or frozen
  corn kernels
4 cups cooked long-grain
  rice

Chicken Fried Rice

Heat the butter in a small heavy-bottom skillet and add the beaten egg. Swirl the egg until it covers the bottom of the skillet. Cook until the egg has set and is cooked through, then turn out onto a plate. Cut the omelet into strips.

Heat a wok over medium heat, then add the oil. Add the shallots and fry until softened, then add the chicken and 2 tablespoons of the soy sauce and stir-fry for 5–6 minutes.

Stir in the carrots, celery, bell pepper, peas, and corn and stir-fry for an additional 5 minutes. Add the rice and stir thoroughly.

Finally, stir in the omelet strips and the remaining soy sauce. Serve immediately.

SERVES 4

1 tbsp peanut or corn oil
2 red onions, sliced
2 tbsp Penang curry paste
1¾ cups canned coconut milk
⅔ cup chicken stock
4 kaffir lime leaves, coarsely torn
1 lemongrass stalk, finely chopped

6 skinless, boneless chicken thighs, chopped
1 tbsp Thai fish sauce
2 tbsp Thai soy sauce
1 tsp jaggery or light brown sugar
½ cup chopped roasted peanuts, plus extra to garnish

1 cup coarsely chopped fresh pineapple
6-inch/15-cm piece cucumber, peeled, halved lengthwise, seeded, and thickly sliced

Penang Chicken Curry

Heat a wok over medium–high heat, then add the oil. Add the onions and stir-fry for 1 minute. Add the curry paste and stir-fry for 1–2 minutes.

Pour in the coconut milk and stock. Add the lime leaves and lemongrass and let simmer for 1 minute. Add the chicken and gradually bring to a boil. Let simmer for 8–10 minutes, until the chicken is tender.

Stir in the fish sauce, soy sauce, and jaggery and let simmer for 1–2 minutes. Stir in the peanuts, pineapple, and cucumber and cook for 30 seconds. Serve immediately, sprinkled with extra peanuts.

SERVES 4

8 oz/225 g dried medium egg noodles

3 tbsp peanut or corn oil

1 large garlic clove, thinly sliced

2 tsp finely chopped fresh ginger

1 lb/450 g turkey steaks, cut into thin pieces

2 cups sliced cremini mushrooms

4 heads of bok choy, stalks chopped into 1-inch/2.5-cm pieces, leaves sliced into wide ribbons

4 scallions, green parts included, diagonally sliced into 1-inch/2.5-cm pieces

1 tbsp light soy sauce

2 tbsp chopped fresh cilantro

salt and pepper

Turkey with Bok Choy & Mushrooms

Cook the noodles according to the package directions, until tender. Drain, rinse, and drain again, then let cool.

Heat a wok over medium–high heat, then add the oil. Stir-fry the garlic and ginger for a few seconds to flavor the oil.

Add the turkey and stir-fry for 2 minutes, until no longer pink. Add the mushrooms and bok choy stalks and stir-fry for 2 minutes. Add the bok choy leaves and the scallions and stir-fry for an additional 2 minutes. Stir in the noodles and soy sauce and season to taste with salt and pepper. Cook until the noodles are heated through, then add the cilantro. Serve immediately.

SERVES 4

2 tbsp peanut or corn oil
1 lb/450 g skinless,
boneless turkey breast,
cut into thin strips

2 tbsp finely chopped
preserved ginger
½ cup fresh or frozen
cranberries

3½ oz/100 g canned
chestnuts
4 tbsp cranberry sauce
3 tbsp light soy sauce
salt and pepper

Stir-Fried Turkey with Cranberry Glaze

Heat a wok over medium–high heat, then add the oil. Add the turkey and stir-fry for
5 minutes, until cooked through.

Add the preserved ginger and cranberries to the wok and cook for 2–3 minutes, or
until the cranberries have started to become soft.

Add the chestnuts, cranberry sauce, and soy sauce, season to taste with salt and
pepper, and bubble for 2–3 minutes.

Transfer to a serving dish and serve immediately.

SERVES 2

generous 1 cup water
½ cup basmati rice
2 tsp peanut or corn oil
1 small egg, beaten
3½ oz/100 g turkey steak,
    cut into thin strips

1 carrot, cut into thin
    lengths
4 scallions, chopped
2 garlic cloves, crushed
1 fresh red chile, seeded
    and chopped

3½ oz/100 g cooked
    peeled shrimp
scant ½ cup fresh bean
    sprouts
2 tsp soy sauce
pinch of superfine sugar

Nasi Goreng

Bring the water to a boil in a pan and add the rice. Return to a boil, then reduce the heat to a simmer. Cover the pan and cook for 10–15 minutes, until the rice is tender and all the water has been absorbed.

Meanwhile, heat 1 teaspoon of the oil in a small heavy-bottom skillet and add the beaten egg. Swirl the egg until it covers the bottom of the skillet. Cook until the egg has set and is cooked through, then turn out onto a plate. Cut the omelet into strips.

When the rice is nearly cooked, heat a wok over high heat, then add the remaining oil. Add the turkey and stir-fry for 1 minute. Add the carrot, scallions, garlic, and chile and stir-fry for an additional 2 minutes.

Reduce the heat, add the cooked rice to the wok with the shrimp, bean sprouts, soy sauce, and sugar and stir gently for 1–2 minutes. If the mixture sticks, add a little water or stock. Arrange the omelet strips on top and serve immediately.

SERVES 4

1 tsp Chinese five-spice powder
1 tbsp cornstarch
4 skinless, boneless duck breasts, cut into thin strips

1 tbsp chili oil
8 oz/225 g pearl onions, peeled
2 garlic cloves, crushed
6 baby corn

1¼ cups canned pineapple chunks
6 scallions, sliced
1 cup fresh bean sprouts
2 tbsp plum sauce

Fruity Duck Stir-Fry

Mix the five-spice powder and the cornstarch. Toss the duck in the mixture until well coated.

Heat a wok over high heat, then add the oil. Cook the duck for 10 minutes, or until just beginning to crispen around the edges. Remove from the wok and set aside.

Add the onions and garlic to the wok and cook for 5 minutes, or until softened. Add the baby corn and cook for an additional 5 minutes. Add the pineapple, scallions, and bean sprouts and cook for 3–4 minutes. Stir in the plum sauce.

Return the cooked duck to the wok and toss until well mixed. Transfer to individual serving dishes and serve immediately.

SERVES 4

2 tbsp honey
4 tbsp soy sauce

4 skinless, boneless duck
breasts, sliced
1 tbsp peanut or corn oil
bunch of scallions, sliced

1 small head of Chinese
cabbage, finely
shredded
salt and pepper

Honeyed Duck Stir-Fry

Mix the honey and soy sauce together in a large bowl. Add the duck slices and toss to coat in the mixture.

Heat a wok over high heat, then add the oil. Add the duck strips, reserving the marinade, and cook quickly for 2 minutes, until browned.

Add the scallions, Chinese cabbage, and the reserved marinade. Cook for 3–4 minutes, until the duck is cooked but still a little pink in the center.

Season to taste with salt and pepper and serve immediately.

Fish & Seafood

SERVES 4–6

½ tsp salt
1 lb/450 g thick whitefish fillets, cut into 1-inch/2.5-cm chunks
2 dried Chinese mushrooms
3 tbsp peanut or corn oil
1-inch/2.5-cm piece fresh ginger, finely shredded

1 tbsp chopped scallion
1 red bell pepper, seeded and cut into 1-inch/2.5-cm squares
1 green bell pepper, seeded and cut into 1-inch/2.5-cm squares

1 oz/25 g canned bamboo shoots, drained and cut into small cubes
2 tsp Chinese rice wine
2 tbsp toasted pine nuts

Fried Fish with Pine Nuts

Sprinkle the salt over the fish and set aside for 20 minutes. Soak the mushrooms in a bowl of warm water for 20 minutes. Squeeze out any excess water from the mushrooms and finely slice, discarding any tough stems.

Heat a wok over medium–high heat, then add 2 tablespoons of the oil. Fry the fish for 3 minutes. Drain and set aside.

Wipe out the wok with paper towels, then add the remaining oil. Toss in the ginger and stir-fry until fragrant. Add the scallion, bell peppers, bamboo shoots, mushrooms, and rice wine and cook for 1–2 minutes.

Finally, add the fish and stir to warm through. Sprinkle over the pine nuts and serve immediately.

SERVES 6

1 cup all-purpose flour
6 catfish, flounder, or
  tilapia fillets, about
  6 oz/175 g each
4–6 tbsp peanut or corn
  oil

2 large garlic cloves,
  thinly sliced
4 ripe tomatoes,
  quartered
1 tbsp Thai fish sauce
12 fresh dill sprigs

12 fresh cilantro sprigs,
12 fresh Thai basil leaves
salt and pepper
cooked rice and Sweet,
  Sour & Spicy Fish Sauce
  (see page 6), to serve

Crispy Fish with Stir-Fried Tomatoes & Herbs

Put the flour in a sealable plastic bag with salt and pepper to taste. Add the fish and seal the bag, then shake to coat each fillet evenly.

Heat 2 tablespoons of the oil in a skillet over high heat. Working in batches and adding extra oil as needed, pan-fry the fillets for 5–7 minutes, or until golden and crisp on both sides. Transfer to a serving platter.

Heat a wok over high heat, then add 1 tablespoon of the oil. Add the garlic and stir-fry for 3–5 minutes, or until just golden. Add the tomatoes and fish sauce and stir-fry for 10 minutes, or until softened. Adjust the seasoning, adding salt and pepper if needed. Spoon the tomato mixture on top of the fish.

Wipe out the wok with paper towels, then heat the remaining tablespoon of oil over high heat. Add the dill, cilantro, and basil and stir-fry for 1–2 minutes, or until just wilted. Scatter the herbs over the tomatoes and fish. Serve with rice and Sweet, Sour, and Spicy Fish Sauce on the side.

SERVES 4

2 tbsp peanut or corn oil
1 garlic clove, chopped
2 tbsp Thai green curry
  paste
1 small eggplant, diced

½ cup canned coconut
  cream
2 tbsp Thai fish sauce
1 tsp jaggery or light
  brown sugar
8 oz/225 g firm whitefish,
  cut into pieces

½ cup fish stock
2 kaffir lime leaves, finely
  shredded
about 15 fresh Thai basil
  leaves
fresh dill sprigs, to garnish

Thai Green Fish Curry

Heat a wok over medium heat, then add the oil. Add the garlic and fry until golden.
Add the curry paste and stir-fry for a few seconds before adding the eggplant. Stir-
fry for about 4–5 minutes, until softened.

Add the coconut cream, bring to a boil, and stir until the cream thickens and
curdles slightly. Add the fish sauce and jaggery to the wok and stir well.

Stir in the fish and stock. Simmer for 3–4 minutes, stirring occasionally, until the fish
is just tender. Add the lime leaves and basil, then cook for an additional minute.
Transfer to individual serving dishes and garnish with dill sprigs. Serve immediately.

SERVES 6

1 lb/450 g fresh bun or 8 oz/225 g dried fine rice noodles
½ cup rice flour or all-purpose flour
½ tsp ground turmeric

2 lb/900 g fish fillets, such as catfish, tilapia, or flounder, cut into ¾-inch/2-cm cubes
2 tbsp peanut or corn oil, plus extra for deep-frying

4 scallions, cut into 1-inch/2.5-cm lengths
⅓ cup dry-roasted unsalted peanuts
24 fresh Thai basil leaves
24 fresh dill sprigs
24 fresh cilantro sprigs
salt and pepper

Rice Noodles with Fried Yellow Fish, Peanuts & Herbs

If the bun has been refrigerated, reheat in boiling water for 2 seconds. Drain the bun and divide among six individual serving dishes. If using rice noodles, cook according to the package directions, until tender. Transfer to individual serving dishes.

Put the flour and turmeric in a sealable plastic bag and season to taste with salt and pepper. Shake to mix well. Add the fish cubes, then seal the bag and shake to coat each fish cube evenly.

Heat enough oil for deep-frying in a saucepan over medium–high heat to 350–375°F/180–190°C, or until a cube of bread browns in 30 seconds. Working in small batches, take a handful of fish cubes and shake off the excess flour, then lower into the hot oil. Deep-fry for 2–3 minutes, or until golden and crisp. Drain on paper towels. Divide the fried fish cubes equally among the dishes.

Heat a wok over high heat, then add the 2 tablespoons of oil. Add the scallions and peanuts and stir-fry for 1 minute. Add the basil, dill, and cilantro and stir-fry for 1–2 minutes, or until just wilted. Divide among the dishes and serve immediately.

SERVES 4

9 oz/250 g dried medium egg noodles
2 tbsp peanut or corn oil, plus extra for brushing
juice and finely grated rind of 1 large lemon
4 whitefish fillets, about 5 oz/140 g each, skinned

paprika, to taste
2 garlic cloves, chopped
1-inch/2.5-cm piece fresh ginger, finely chopped
2 tbsp very finely chopped fresh cilantro root
1 tbsp kecap manis (sweet soy sauce)

1 fresh red Thai chile, seeded and finely chopped
1 tbsp Thai fish sauce
salt and pepper

Fish with Spiced Noodles

Preheat the broiler to high. Put the noodles in a pan of boiling water and cook for 3 minutes, or cook according to the package directions, until tender. Drain, rinse with cold water, and drain again, then set aside.

Mix 1 tablespoon of the oil with the lemon juice and brush over one side of each fish fillet. Sprinkle with the lemon rind and paprika and season to taste with salt and pepper. Lightly brush the broiler rack with oil, then place the fish on the rack and cook under the preheated broiler for 8–10 minutes, until the flesh flakes easily.

Meanwhile, heat a wok over high heat, then add the remaining oil. Add the garlic and ginger and stir-fry for about 30 seconds. Add the cilantro root and kecap manis and stir around. Add the noodles and stir thoroughly so they are coated in the kecap manis. Stir in the chile and fish sauce. Divide the spiced noodles among individual serving plates, top each with a fish fillet, and serve immediately.

SERVES 4

2 tsp peanut or corn oil
1 lb/450 g monkfish fillets, cut into 1-inch/2.5-cm chunks
1 onion, thinly sliced

3 garlic cloves, finely chopped
1 tsp grated fresh ginger
8 oz/225 g fine asparagus

3 cups thinly sliced mushrooms
2 tbsp light soy sauce
1 tbsp lemon juice

Monkfish Stir-Fry

Heat a wok over medium–high heat, then add the oil. Add the fish, onion, garlic, ginger, asparagus, and mushrooms. Stir-fry for 2–3 minutes.

Stir in the soy sauce and lemon juice and cook for an additional minute. Remove from the heat and transfer to individual dishes. Serve immediately.

SERVES 4

4 monkfish fillets, about 115 g/4 oz each
¼ cup rice flour or cornstarch
6 tbsp peanut or corn oil

4 garlic cloves, crushed
2 large fresh red chiles, seeded and sliced
2 tsp jaggery or light brown sugar

juice of 2 limes
grated rind of 1 lime
2–3 tbsp water
cooked rice and lime wedges, to serve

Monkfish with Lime & Chile Sauce

Toss the fish in the flour, shaking off any excess. Heat a wok over medium–high heat, then add the oil. Cook the fish on all sides until browned and cooked through, being careful when turning not to break it up.

Lift the fish out of the wok and keep warm. Add the garlic and chiles and stir-fry for 1–2 minutes, until they have softened.

Add the jaggery, the lime juice and rind, and water and bring to a boil. Let simmer gently for 1–2 minutes, then spoon the mixture over the fish. Serve immediately with rice and lime wedges.

SERVES 4

4 tuna steaks, about
4 oz/115 g each, cut
into strips
8 oz/225 g dried medium
egg noodles
1 tbsp toasted sesame
seeds
2 scallions, diagonally
sliced

marinade
½ cup teriyaki sauce
2 tsp honey
salt and pepper

stir-fry
1 tbsp peanut or corn oil
2 tsp sesame oil
1 carrot, cut into thin
strips

2 heads of bok choy,
stalks and leaves
separated and finely
sliced
1 yellow bell pepper,
seeded and cut into
thin strips
2 garlic cloves, chopped
1 tbsp soy sauce

Teriyaki Tuna with Stir-Fried Vegetables & Noodles

For the marinade, mix together the teriyaki sauce, honey, and salt and pepper to taste in a shallow dish. Add the tuna and turn to coat in the marinade. Cover with plastic wrap and let marinate in the refrigerator for 1 hour, turning the tuna occasionally.

Cook the noodles according to the package directions, until tender. Drain well and set aside.

Meanwhile, preheat the broiler to high. Line the broiler pan with aluminum foil. Remove the tuna from the marinade, reserving the marinade, and arrange in the broiler pan. Spoon over half the marinade and cook under the preheated broiler for 1 minute. Turn over, spoon over the remaining marinade, and cook for an additional minute.

Heat a wok over high heat, then add the oils. Stir-fry the carrot, bok choy stalks, and bell pepper for 2 minutes. Add the garlic and bok choy leaves and stir-fry for 1 minute. Add the soy sauce and a little water. Divide the noodles among four individual serving bowls. Top with the stir-fried vegetables, tuna, and any cooking juices, and sprinkle with the sesame seeds and scallions. Serve immediately.

SERVES 4

1 lb/450 g salmon fillet, skinned
2 tbsp kecap manis (sweet soy sauce)
2 tbsp ketchup

1 tsp rice vinegar
1 tbsp raw brown sugar
1 garlic clove, crushed
4 tbsp peanut or corn oil

1 lb/450 g leeks, thinly shredded
sliced fresh red chiles, to garnish

Stir-Fried Salmon with Leeks

Using a sharp knife, cut the salmon into slices. Place the slices of salmon in a shallow nonmetallic dish.

Mix together the kecap manis, ketchup, vinegar, sugar, and garlic in a small bowl. Pour the mixture over the salmon, toss well, and let marinate for about 30 minutes.

Meanwhile, heat a wok over medium–high heat, then add 3 tablespoons of the oil. Add the leeks to the wok and stir-fry for about 10 minutes, or until the leeks become crispy and tender.

Using a slotted spoon, carefully remove the leeks from the wok and transfer to warmed serving plates.

Add the remaining oil to the wok. Add the salmon and the marinade to the wok and cook for 2 minutes. Remove the salmon from the wok and arrange on top of the leeks. Garnish with chiles and serve immediately.

SERVES 4

8 baby corn
2 tbsp peanut or corn oil
1 red onion, sliced
1 orange bell pepper,
  seeded and sliced
1 green bell pepper,
  seeded and sliced

1 lb/450 g salmon fillet,
  skinned
1 tbsp paprika
1⅓ cups pineapple
  chunks
generous ¾ cup fresh
  bean sprouts

2 tbsp ketchup
2 tbsp soy sauce
2 tbsp Chinese rice wine
  or dry sherry
1 tsp cornstarch

Stir-Fried Salmon with Pineapple

Cut each baby corn in half. Heat a wok over medium–high heat, then add the oil. Add the onion, bell peppers, and baby corn to the wok and stir-fry for 5 minutes.

Cut the salmon into thin strips and place in a large bowl. Sprinkle with the paprika and toss well to coat.

Add the salmon to the wok together with the pineapple and stir-fry for an additional 2–3 minutes, or until the fish is tender. Add the bean sprouts to the wok and toss well.

Mix together the ketchup, soy sauce, rice wine, and cornstarch. Add to the wok and cook until the juices start to thicken. Transfer to serving dishes and serve immediately.

SERVES 4

1½ tbsp peanut or corn oil

1⅓ cups snow peas

12 baby corn

1 large orange or yellow bell pepper, seeded and thinly sliced

8 scallions, halved lengthwise

2 garlic cloves, crushed

¾-inch/2-cm piece fresh ginger, finely chopped

2 tbsp teriyaki marinade

¾ cup cashew nuts

14 oz/400 g large cooked peeled jumbo shrimp

1 tbsp sesame oil

Teriyaki Shrimp with Cashew Nuts

Heat a wok over high heat, then add the oil. Add all the vegetables and stir-fry for 4 minutes, or until almost tender but still with a bite. Add the garlic and ginger and stir-fry for 1 minute.

Add the teriyaki marinade, cashew nuts, and shrimp and stir-fry for 2 minutes.

Transfer to serving bowls, drizzle over the sesame oil, and serve immediately.

SERVES 2

1 tbsp peanut or corn oil
4 oz/115 g large shrimp,
  peeled and deveined

4 eggs, lightly beaten
1 tsp salt
pinch of white pepper

2 tbsp snipped fresh
  garlic chives, plus extra
  to garnish

Shrimp Fu Yung

Heat a wok over medium–high heat, then add the oil. Add the shrimp and stir-fry for about 4 minutes, until they begin to turn pink.

Season the eggs with the salt and pepper and pour over the shrimp. Stir-fry for 1 minute, then add the garlic chives.

Cook for an additional 4 minutes, stirring all the time, until the eggs are cooked through but still soft in texture. Serve immediately, garnished with extra garlic chives.

SERVES 2

12 oz/350 g jumbo
  shrimp
1½ tbsp finely chopped
  fresh ginger
2 shallots, finely chopped

½ fresh green chile,
  seeded and finely
  chopped
4 tbsp peanut or corn oil
3 tbsp chopped fresh
  cilantro
cooked rice, to serve

tamarind sauce
1 tbsp tamarind paste
1 tbsp sugar
2 tsp oyster sauce
2 tbsp water
1 tsp Thai fish sauce

Jumbo Shrimp in Tamarind Sauce

Remove the heads and shells from the shrimp, leaving the tails intact, and devein.
In a small bowl, combine the ginger, shallots, and chile. Combine the sauce
ingredients in a separate bowl.

Heat a wok over medium–high heat, then add the oil. When the oil is almost
smoking, add the shrimp and stir-fry for 3–4 minutes, until they begin to turn pink.
Remove from the wok and drain in a colander.

Pour off all but 2 tablespoons of oil from the wok. Stir-fry the ginger mixture for
1 minute. Add the sauce and stir for a few seconds, until hot. Add the shrimp and
stir-fry for 1 minute, until the sauce is slightly reduced.

Transfer the shrimp to individual serving dishes and sprinkle over the cilantro. Serve
immediately with rice.

SERVES 4

12 oz/350 g jumbo shrimp
2 tbsp peanut or corn oil
1–2 garlic cloves, crushed
bunch of scallions, chopped

snipped fresh garlic chives, to garnish
lime wedges, to serve

chile dipping sauce
2 tbsp molasses
6 tbsp rice vinegar

2 tbsp Thai fish sauce or light soy sauce
2 tbsp water
1 garlic clove, crushed
2 tsp grated fresh ginger
2 tsp finely chopped fresh red chile

Garlic-Sizzled Shrimp with Chile Dipping Sauce

Remove the heads and shells from the shrimp, leaving the tails intact, and devein.

To make the sauce, heat the molasses, vinegar, fish sauce, and water in a small pan until boiling. Add the garlic, ginger, and chile and pour into a small serving bowl.

Heat a wok over high heat, then add the oil. Add the garlic and scallions and stir-fry for 2 minutes, then add the shrimp and cook for an additional 2–3 minutes, until they have turned pink.

Transfer to a serving plate, garnish with garlic chives, and serve with the chile dipping sauce and lime wedges.

SERVES 4

3 tbsp peanut or corn oil
2 tbsp sesame oil
16 large scallops, halved
8 oz/225 g small shiitake
  mushrooms, tough
  stems removed

1½ cups snow peas,
  diagonally halved
2 tsp finely chopped fresh
  ginger
2 garlic cloves, finely
  chopped

2 tsp light soy sauce
juice of 1 lime
3 tbsp torn fresh cilantro
salt and pepper

Scallop, Snow Peas & Mushroom Stir-Fry

Heat a wok over high heat, then add the oils. Stir-fry the scallops for 1 minute. Add the mushrooms and snow peas and stir-fry for an additional minute.

Add the ginger, garlic, soy sauce, and a splash of water to moisten. Stir-fry for an additional 1–2 minutes, until the vegetables are just tender.

Add the lime juice and cilantro and season to taste with salt and pepper. Divide among serving plates and serve immediately.

SERVES 4

1 tsp peanut or corn oil
2-inch/5-cm piece fresh ginger, grated
1 tbsp finely grated lime rind
1 orange bell pepper, seeded and sliced

1 red onion, thinly sliced
10½ oz/300 g scallops
4 oz/115 g wild mushrooms, such as chanterelle or cremini mushrooms

¼ cup lime juice
1 tsp honey (optional)
1 tbsp soy sauce
1 head of bok choy, shredded

Scallop Stir-Fry

Heat a wok over high heat, then add the oil. Add the ginger and cook, stirring, for 1 minute.

Add the lime rind, bell pepper, and onion and stir-fry for 3–4 minutes, or until the onion has softened.

Add the scallops and mushrooms to the wok and stir-fry for 2 minutes. Pour in the lime juice, add the honey, if using, and the soy sauce. Stir together, then add the bok choy and continue to cook for 2–3 minutes, or until the scallops are tender. Serve immediately.

SERVES 2

2 lb/900 g small clams, scrubbed

1 tbsp peanut or corn oil

1 tsp finely chopped fresh ginger

1 tsp finely chopped garlic

1 tbsp fermented black beans, rinsed and coarsely chopped

2 tsp Chinese rice wine

1 tbsp finely chopped scallion

1 tsp salt (optional)

Clams in Black Bean Sauce

Discard any clams with broken shells and any that refuse to close when tapped. Set aside the remaining clams.

Heat a wok with a lid over high heat, then add the oil. Stir-fry the ginger and garlic until fragrant. Add the black beans and cook for 1 minute.

Add the clams and rice wine and stir-fry for 2 minutes to combine all the ingredients. Cover and cook for about 3 minutes, or until the clams have opened. Discard any clams that remain closed. Stir in the scallion and the salt, if using. Serve immediately.

SERVES 4

1 lb 10 oz/750 g squid, cleaned and tentacles discarded
1 large red bell pepper, seeded
scant 1 cup snow peas
1 head of bok choy

1 tbsp peanut or corn oil
1 small fresh red Thai chile, chopped
1 garlic clove, finely chopped
1 tsp grated fresh ginger
2 scallions, chopped

sauce
3 tbsp black bean sauce
1 tbsp Thai fish sauce
1 tbsp Chinese rice wine or dry sherry
1 tbsp dark soy sauce
1 tsp brown sugar
1 tsp cornstarch
1 tbsp water

Stir-Fried Squid with Hot Black Bean Sauce

Cut the squid body cavities lengthwise into quarters. Use the tip of a small, sharp knife to score a diamond pattern into the flesh without cutting all the way through. Pat dry with paper towels.

Cut the bell pepper into long, thin slices. Cut the snow peas in half diagonally. Coarsely shred the bok choy.

To make the sauce, mix the black bean sauce, fish sauce, rice wine, soy sauce, and sugar in a bowl. Blend the cornstarch with the water and stir into the other ingredients in the bowl. Set aside.

Heat a wok over high heat, then add the oil. Add the chile, garlic, ginger, and scallions and stir-fry for 1 minute. Add the bell pepper slices and stir-fry for 2 minutes.

Add the squid and stir-fry for an additional minute. Stir in the snow peas and bok choy and cook for an additional minute, or until wilted.

Stir in the sauce and cook, stirring constantly, for 2 minutes, or until the sauce thickens and clears. Serve immediately on warmed plates.

SERVES 4

3 tbsp peanut or corn oil
2 large fresh crabs,
    cleaned, broken
    into pieces and legs
    cracked with a cleaver

1½-inch/4-cm piece
    fresh ginger, cut into
    julienne strips
bunch of scallions,
    chopped into 2-inch/
    5-cm lengths

2 tbsp light soy sauce
1 tsp sugar
pinch of white pepper

Stir-Fried Fresh Crab with Ginger

Heat a wok with a lid over high heat, then add 2 tablespoons of the oil. Stir-fry the crab for 3–4 minutes. Remove from the wok and set aside.

Heat the remaining oil in the wok, add the ginger, and stir until fragrant. Add the scallions, then stir in the crab pieces. Add the soy sauce, sugar, and pepper. Cover and simmer for 1 minute. Serve immediately.

SERVES 4

2 tbsp peanut or corn oil
1 large onion, chopped
1 garlic clove, finely
  chopped
8 large tomatoes, peeled,
  seeded, and chopped

generous 1 cup paella or
  risotto rice
about 3½ cups fish stock
1 lb/450 g mussels,
  scrubbed and
  debearded
14 oz/400 g frozen mixed
  seafood, thawed

1½ cups cooked young
  peas
2 tbsp chopped fresh
  cilantro
salt and pepper

Quick Seafood Rice

Heat a wok over high heat, then add the oil. Add the onion and cook until just
softened. Add the garlic and half the tomatoes and stir together well. Add the rice
and stir-fry for 2–3 minutes, then add half the stock and bring to a boil. Let simmer
for 12–15 minutes, adding more stock as necessary.

Discard any mussels with broken shells and any that refuse to close when tapped.
Add the remaining mussels to the wok with the mixed seafood and peas. Season
to taste with salt and pepper and cook for an additional 3–4 minutes, until hot,
the mussels have opened, and the liquid has been mostly absorbed. Discard any
mussels that remain closed.

Stir in the remaining tomatoes, then taste and adjust the seasoning, adding salt
and pepper if needed. Sprinkle over the cilantro and serve immediately.

SERVES 4

4 oz/115 g whitefish fillets
2 tbsp peanut or corn oil
1 fresh jalapeño chile,
  seeded and finely
  chopped
1-inch/2.5-cm piece fresh
  ginger, grated

3 oz/85 g shrimp, peeled
  and deveined
8 baby corn, halved
  lengthwise
1 cup snow peas
6 scallions, chopped

1 tbsp soy sauce
4 oz/115 g squid,
  cleaned and cut into
  thin slices
2½ cups spinach leaves
¾ cup fresh bean sprouts

Seafood Stir-Fry

Discard any skin from the fish, rinse lightly, and pat dry on paper towels. Cut into small pieces.

Heat a wok over high heat, then add the oil. Add the chile and ginger and stir-fry for 1 minute, then add the fish and shrimp and stir-fry for 2 minutes.

Add the baby corn, snow peas, scallions, and soy sauce and continue to stir-fry for 2–3 minutes, or until the fish is just cooked and the shrimp have started to turn pink.

Add the squid, spinach, and bean sprouts and continue to stir-fry for an additional 2 minutes, or until the fish, shrimp, and squid are cooked. Serve immediately.

SERVES 4

7 oz/200 g squid, cleaned and tentacles discarded

1 lb 2 oz/500 g firm whitefish fillets

12 clams, scrubbed

1 tbsp peanut or corn oil

4 shallots, finely chopped

2 garlic cloves, finely chopped

2 tbsp Thai green curry paste

2 small lemongrass stalks, finely chopped

1 tsp shrimp paste

generous 2 cups canned coconut milk

7 oz/200 g jumbo shrimp, peeled and deveined

8 fresh basil leaves, finely shredded, plus extra leaves to garnish

Spicy Thai Seafood Stew

Using a sharp knife, cut the squid body cavities into thick rings and the fish into bite-size chunks. Discard any clams with broken shells and any that refuse to close when tapped.

Heat a wok over medium–high heat, then add the oil. Add the shallots, garlic, and curry paste and stir-fry for 1–2 minutes. Add the lemongrass and shrimp paste, then stir in the coconut milk and bring to a boil.

Reduce the heat until the liquid is simmering gently, then add the squid, fish, and shrimp to the wok and simmer for 2 minutes.

Add the clams and simmer for an additional minute, or until the clams have opened. Discard any clams that remain closed.

Sprinkle the shredded basil over the stew. Transfer to individual serving plates, then garnish with basil leaves and serve immediately.

SERVES 4

4 oz/115 g dried wide rice noodles
2 tbsp peanut or corn oil
6 scallions, cut into 1-inch/2.5-cm lengths
1 large carrot, cut into thin sticks
½ cup sliced green beans

2 tbsp Thai red curry paste
3 cups canned coconut milk
8 oz/225 g skinned whitefish fillet, cut into 1-inch/2.5-cm cubes
8 oz/225 g squid, cleaned and cut into thick rings

8 oz/225 g large shrimp, peeled and deveined
⅓ cup fresh bean sprouts
handful of fresh cilantro, chopped
fresh Thai basil leaves, to garnish

Mixed Fish & Coconut Curry

Cook the noodles according to the package directions, until tender. Drain well and set aside.

Heat a wok over medium–high heat, then add the oil. Add the scallions, carrot, and green beans and stir-fry for 2–3 minutes, or until starting to soften.

Stir in the curry paste, then add the coconut milk. Bring gently to a boil, stirring occasionally, then reduce the heat and simmer for 2–3 minutes. Add the fish, squid, shrimp, and bean sprouts and simmer for 2–3 minutes, or until just cooked through and the shrimp have turned pink.

Stir in the noodles and cilantro and cook for 1 minute. Serve immediately, garnished with the basil.

Vegetables

SERVES 2

1 butternut squash, weighing about 1 lb 2 oz/500 g
6 large shiitake mushrooms
5 tbsp peanut or corn oil
½ tsp white peppercorns, crushed

½ tsp coriander seeds, crushed
2 large garlic cloves, thinly sliced
finely grated rind of ½ lemon
½ tbsp rice vinegar

4 tbsp chicken or vegetable stock
2 handfuls of baby spinach, stalks removed
salt

Stir-Fried Butternut Squash

Slice the squash crosswise at the point where the rounded part meets the neck. Remove the skin from each piece. Quarter the rounded part and remove the seeds and fibers. Slice lengthwise into thin segments. Slice the neck in half lengthwise, then crosswise into thin semicircles.

Remove and discard the tough stems from the mushrooms and thinly slice the caps.

Heat a wok over medium–high heat, then add the oil. Add half the crushed peppercorns and half the coriander seeds. Stir for a few seconds, then add the squash in small batches. Fry for 5–7 minutes, carefully turning with tongs, until lightly browned and just tender. Season to taste with salt. Using a slotted spoon, transfer to a large strainer set over a bowl.

Add the mushrooms to the wok and fry for 4–5 minutes. Add the garlic and lemon rind and fry for an additional minute. Season to taste with salt and add the remaining peppercorns and coriander seeds. Add to the squash.

Pour any oil drained from the vegetables into the wok. Stir in the vinegar and stock and simmer for a few seconds, until slightly reduced.

Arrange the spinach in individual serving bowls. Pile the vegetables on top, then pour over the juices from the wok. Serve immediately.

SERVES 4

2 tbsp peanut oil or vegetable oil
2 onions, thinly sliced
bunch of fine asparagus spears
1¾ cups canned coconut milk

2 tbsp Thai red curry paste
3 fresh kaffir lime leaves
5 cups baby spinach leaves
2 heads of bok choy, chopped

1 small head of Chinese cabbage, shredded
handful of fresh cilantro, chopped
cooked rice, to serve

Thai Red Curry with Mixed Leaves

Heat a wok over medium–high heat, then add the oil. Add the onions and asparagus and stir-fry for 1–2 minutes.

Add the coconut milk, curry paste, and lime leaves and bring gently to a boil, stirring occasionally. Add the spinach, bok choy, and Chinese cabbage and cook, stirring, for 2–3 minutes, or until wilted. Add the cilantro and stir well. Serve immediately with rice.

SERVES 4

4 tbsp peanut or corn oil
2 garlic cloves, chopped
1 onion, sliced
8 baby corn, halved
  diagonally
½ cucumber, peeled,
  halved, seeded, and
  sliced

8 oz/225 g canned water
  chestnuts, drained
¾ cup snow peas
2 cups shiitake
  mushrooms, halved
1 red bell pepper, seeded
  and thinly sliced

1 tbsp jaggery or light
  brown sugar
2 tbsp Thai soy sauce
1 tbsp Thai fish sauce
1 tbsp rice vinegar
8–12 fresh Thai basil
  sprigs
cooked rice, to serve

Mixed Vegetables with Quick-Fried Basil

Heat a wok over medium–high heat, then add half the oil. Stir-fry the garlic and onion for 1–2 minutes. Add the baby corn, cucumber, water chestnuts, snow peas, mushrooms, and red bell pepper and stir-fry for 2–3 minutes, until starting to soften.

Add the jaggery, soy sauce, fish sauce, and vinegar and gradually bring to a boil. Let simmer for 1–2 minutes.

Meanwhile, heat a separate wok over high heat, then add the remaining oil. Add the basil sprigs and cook for 20–30 seconds, until crisp. Remove with a slotted spoon and drain on paper towels.

Transfer the vegetable stir-fry to serving plates and garnish with the crispy basil. Serve immediately with rice.

SERVES 4

2 tbsp peanut or corn oil
8 scallions, chopped
1 garlic clove, crushed
1 tbsp grated fresh ginger
1 head of broccoli, cut
    into florets

1 yellow or orange bell
    pepper, seeded and
    coarsely chopped
1 cup shredded red
    cabbage
8 baby corn

2 cups thinly sliced
    portobello mushrooms
1⅓ cups fresh bean
    sprouts
9 oz/250 g canned water
    chestnuts, drained
4 tsp light soy sauce

Classic Stir-Fried Vegetables

Heat a wok over high heat, then add the oil. Stir-fry two thirds of the scallions with the garlic and ginger for 30 seconds.

Add the broccoli, bell pepper, and red cabbage and stir-fry for 1–2 minutes. Mix in the baby corn and mushrooms and stir-fry for an additional 1–2 minutes.

Finally, add the bean sprouts and water chestnuts and cook for an additional 2 minutes. Pour in the soy sauce and stir well.

Transfer to warmed dishes and serve immediately, garnished with the remaining scallions.

SERVES 4

1 lb 10 oz/750 g fresh kale
2 tbsp peanut or corn oil
1 onion, chopped
4 large garlic cloves, finely chopped
2 red bell peppers, seeded and thinly sliced

1 large carrot, coarsely grated
1⅓ cups broccoli florets
pinch dried chile flakes (optional)
½ cup vegetable stock

4 oz/115 g sprouted beans
handful of toasted cashews, chopped
salt and pepper
lemon wedges, to serve

Kale Stir-Fry

Using a sharp knife, remove any thick central cores from the kale. Stack several leaves on top of each other, then cut across them to finely shred; repeat until all the kale is shredded. Set aside.

Heat a wok with a lid over high heat, then add the oil. Add the onion and stir-fry for about 3 minutes, then add the garlic, bell peppers, and carrot and continue stir-frying until the onion is tender and the bell peppers are starting to soften.

Add the broccoli and chile flakes, if using, and stir. Add the kale and stir. Add the stock and salt and pepper to taste, reduce the heat to medium, cover the wok, and simmer for about 5 minutes, until the kale is tender.

Remove the lid and let any excess liquid evaporate. Use two forks to mix the sprouted beans through the other ingredients, then adjust the seasoning, adding salt and pepper if needed. Transfer to individual serving plates and sprinkle over the cashew nuts. Serve immediately with lemon wedges.

SERVES 2–3

2 tbsp sesame oil
3 tbsp peanut or corn oil
7 oz/200 g small shiitake
   mushrooms
2 heads of bok choy,
   leaves left whole, stalks
   sliced

1⅓ cups snow peas,
   halved diagonally
9 oz/250 g tofu, drained
   and cubed
1¼-inch/3-cm piece fresh
   ginger, thinly sliced

2 garlic cloves, finely
   chopped
1 tbsp soy sauce
1 tsp sesame seeds
salt and pepper
cooked noodles, to serve

Snow Pea, Sesame & Tofu Stir-Fry

Heat a wok with a lid over medium–high heat, then add the oils. Add the mushrooms, bok choy stalks, and snow peas and stir-fry for 1 minute.

Add the tofu, bok choy leaves, ginger, garlic, and a splash of water to moisten. Stir-fry for an additional 1–2 minutes, until the bok choy leaves have wilted.

Stir in the soy sauce, sprinkle with the sesame seeds, and season to taste with salt and pepper. Serve immediately with noodles.

SERVES 4

1 onion, coarsely chopped
3 garlic cloves, thinly sliced
1-inch/2.5-cm piece fresh ginger, thinly sliced
2 fresh green chiles, seeded and finely chopped

1 tbsp peanut or corn oil
1 tsp ground turmeric
1 tsp ground coriander
1 tsp ground cumin
2 lb 4 oz/1 kg mixed vegetables, such as cauliflower, zucchini, potatoes, carrots, and green beans, cut into chunks

scant 1 cup coconut cream or canned coconut milk
salt and pepper
2 tbsp chopped fresh cilantro, to garnish
cooked rice, to serve

Vegetable & Coconut Curry

Put the onion, garlic, ginger, and chiles in a food processor and process until almost smooth.

Heat a wok with a lid over medium heat, then add the oil. Add the onion mixture, and cook, stirring constantly, for 5 minutes.

Add the turmeric, coriander, and cumin and cook, stirring frequently, for 3–4 minutes. Add the vegetables and stir to coat in the spice paste.

Add the coconut cream to the vegetables, cover, and let simmer for 30–40 minutes, until the vegetables are tender.

Season to taste with salt and pepper, garnish with the cilantro, and serve with rice.

SERVES 4

2 tbsp peanut or vegetable oil
2 shallots, chopped
2 garlic cloves, crushed
generous 1 cup basmati rice
about 2½ cups chicken stock

1 tbsp Thai red curry paste
1 tsp Thai fish sauce
3 tbsp soy sauce
12 baby corn, halved lengthwise
8 baby carrots, halved lengthwise

1 cup snow peas
⅓ cup fresh bean sprouts
4 tbsp sesame seeds
handful of fresh cilantro, chopped
2 tbsp sesame oil
salt

Spring Vegetable Rice

Heat a wok over medium–high heat, then add the peanut oil. Add the shallots and garlic and stir-fry for 1–2 minutes. Add the rice and stir-fry for 2–3 minutes.

Add the stock, curry paste, fish sauce, and soy sauce and bring to a boil, stirring occasionally. Reduce the heat and simmer for 10–12 minutes, or until the rice is tender, adding more stock or boiling water if needed.

Meanwhile, cook the baby corn and carrots in a pan of lightly salted boiling water for 2–3 minutes, or until just tender. Add the snow peas and cook for 1 minute. Add the bean sprouts and stir well, then drain.

Heat a dry skillet until hot, then add the sesame seeds and cook over medium–high heat, shaking the skillet frequently, for 30–45 seconds, or until lightly browned.

Add the drained vegetables, cilantro, and sesame oil to the rice and mix well. Serve immediately, sprinkled with the toasted sesame seeds.

SERVES 4

⅔ cup vegetable stock
1-inch/2.5-cm piece fresh
galangal, sliced
2 garlic cloves, chopped
1 lemongrass stalk
(white part only), finely
chopped

2 fresh red chiles, seeded
and chopped
4 carrots, cut into chunks
2 cups pumpkin cubes
2 tbsp peanut or corn oil
2 shallots, finely chopped

3 tbsp Thai yellow curry
paste
1¾ cups canned
coconut milk
4–6 fresh Thai basil sprigs
2 tbsp toasted pumpkin
seeds, to garnish

Carrot & Pumpkin Curry

Pour the stock into a large pan and bring to a boil. Add the galangal, half the garlic, the lemongrass, and chiles and let simmer for 5 minutes. Add the carrots and pumpkin and let simmer for 5–6 minutes, until tender.

Meanwhile, heat a wok over medium–high heat, then add the oil. Stir-fry the shallots and the remaining garlic for 2–3 minutes. Add the curry paste and stir-fry for 1–2 minutes.

Stir the shallot mixture into the pan and add the coconut milk and Thai basil. Let simmer for 2–3 minutes. Transfer to individual serving bowls and serve immediately, sprinkled with the toasted pumpkin seeds.

SERVES 2

1½ tbsp light soy sauce
1 tbsp oyster sauce
2 tbsp chicken stock or
    Basic Chinese Stock
    (see page 9)
peanut or corn oil, for
    deep-frying

12 oz/350 g firm tofu,
    cubed
2 large garlic cloves,
    thinly sliced
1 cup snow peas,
    diagonally halved
4 scallions, diagonally
    sliced into 1-inch/
    2.5-cm pieces

1 cup fresh bean sprouts
½ bunch fresh garlic
    chives, snipped into
    1-inch/2.5-cm lengths
a few drops of sesame oil
salt and pepper

Stir-Fried Tofu with Bean Sprouts

Combine the soy sauce, oyster sauce, and stock in a small bowl and set aside.

Heat enough peanut oil for deep-frying in a wok to 350–375°F/180–190°C, or until a cube of bread browns in 30 seconds. Add the tofu and deep-fry for 5–7 minutes, until golden brown, turning with tongs. Remove with a slotted spoon and drain on paper towels. Season to taste with salt and pepper.

Drain the oil from the wok, reserving 1 tablespoon, and wipe out the wok with paper towels. Heat the reserved oil, add the garlic, and stir-fry for a few seconds to flavor the oil. Add the snow peas and scallions and stir-fry for 2 minutes.

Add the bean sprouts and soy sauce mixture. Stir-fry for 1 minute, then add the fried tofu and stir to mix. Transfer to individual serving bowls and scatter over the garlic chives. Drizzle with the sesame oil and serve immediately.

SERVES 2

5 oz/140 g dried wide rice noodles
6 tbsp soy sauce
2 tbsp lemon juice
1 tsp granulated sugar

½ tsp cornstarch
1 tbsp peanut or corn oil
2 tsp grated fresh ginger
2 garlic cloves, chopped
4–5 scallions, sliced

2 tbsp Chinese rice wine or dry sherry
7 oz/200 g canned water chestnuts, drained and sliced

Noodle Stir-Fry

Put the noodles in a large bowl, cover with boiling water, and soak for 4 minutes, or cook according to the package directions, until tender. Drain well.

Mix the soy sauce, lemon juice, sugar, and cornstarch in a small bowl.

Heat a wok over medium–high heat, then add the oil. Add the ginger and garlic and stir-fry for 1 minute. Add the scallions and stir-fry for 3 minutes.

Add the rice wine, followed by the soy sauce mixture, and cook for 1 minute.

Stir in the water chestnuts and noodles and cook for an additional 1–2 minutes, or until heated through. Serve immediately.

SERVES 4

2 tbsp peanut or corn oil
6 scallions, sliced
3 garlic cloves, crushed
1 red bell pepper, seeded
  and diced
1 green bell pepper,
  seeded and diced

1 fresh red chile, seeded
  and sliced
2 tbsp chopped water
  chestnuts
1 zucchini, chopped
4½ oz/125 g oyster
  mushrooms

3 tbsp black bean sauce
2 tsp Chinese rice wine or
  dry sherry
4 tbsp dark soy sauce
1 tsp dark brown sugar
2 tbsp water
1 tsp sesame oil

Eight-Jewel Vegetables

Heat a wok over high heat, then add the peanut oil. Reduce the heat slightly, add the scallions and garlic, and stir-fry for about 30 seconds.

Add the bell peppers, chile, water chestnuts, and zucchini to the wok and stir-fry for 2–3 minutes, or until the vegetables are just beginning to soften.

Add the mushrooms, black bean sauce, rice wine, soy sauce, sugar, and water to the wok and stir-fry for an additional 4 minutes.

Drizzle over the sesame oil and serve immediately.

SERVES 4

2 tbsp peanut or corn oil
2¼ cups grated carrots
8 oz/225 g leeks,
    shredded

2 oranges, peeled and
    segmented
2 tbsp ketchup
1 tbsp raw brown sugar

2 tbsp light soy sauce
½ cup chopped peanuts

Carrot + Orange Stir-Fry

Heat a wok over high heat, then add the oil. Add the carrots and leeks to the wok and stir-fry for 2–3 minutes, or until the vegetables are just soft.

Add the orange segments to the wok and heat through gently, ensuring that you do not break up the orange segments as you stir the mixture.

Mix the ketchup, brown sugar, and soy sauce in a small bowl. Add the ketchup mixture to the wok and cook for an additional 2 minutes.

Transfer the stir-fry to individual serving bowls and scatter with the peanuts. Serve immediately.

SERVES 4

6 dried Chinese mushrooms
9½ oz/275 g firm tofu, drained
3 tbsp peanut or corn oil, plus extra for deep-frying
1 carrot, cut into thin strips

1½ cups snow peas
10–12 baby corn, halved lengthwise
8 oz/225 g canned bamboo shoots, drained and sliced
1 red bell pepper, seeded and cut into chunks
1 cup shredded Chinese cabbage

1 tbsp soy sauce
1 tbsp black bean sauce
1 tsp sugar
1 tsp cornstarch
9 oz/250 g dried fine rice noodles, broken into 3-inch/7.5-cm lengths
salt

Crispy Noodle, Vegetable & Tofu Stir-Fry

Soak the mushrooms in a bowl of warm water for 20 minutes. Drain, reserving the soaking liquid. Squeeze out the excess water from the mushrooms and slice thinly, discarding any tough stems.

Cut the tofu into cubes, then boil in a pan of lightly salted water for 2–3 minutes to firm up. Drain well. Heat a wok with a lid over medium–high heat, then add 1½ tablespoons of the oil. Add the tofu and fry until lightly browned. Remove and drain on paper towels.

Add the remaining 1½ tablespoons of the oil to the wok and stir-fry the mushrooms, carrot, snow peas, baby corn, bamboo shoots, and bell pepper for 2–3 minutes. Add the Chinese cabbage and tofu and continue to stir-fry for an additional 2 minutes. Stir in the soy sauce, black bean sauce, and sugar.

Combine 6 tablespoons of the reserved mushroom liquid with the cornstarch, then add to the wok. Bring to a boil, reduce the heat, cover, and simmer for 2–3 minutes, until the sauce thickens slightly.

Heat enough oil for deep-frying in a wok to 350–375°F/180–190°C, or until a cube of bread browns in 30 seconds. Deep-fry the noodles, in batches, for 1½–2 minutes, or until crisp and puffed up. Drain on paper towels and serve with the stir-fry.

SERVES 4

2 eggplants, peeled
6 tbsp peanut or corn oil
2 red bell peppers, seeded and thinly sliced
8 oz/225 g canned water chestnuts, drained and sliced
6 scallions, sliced
2 tsp finely chopped fresh ginger

1 large garlic clove, thinly sliced
1 fresh green chile, seeded and finely chopped
²/₃ cup hot vegetable stock
sesame seeds and thinly sliced scallions, to garnish

sauce
1½ tbsp soy sauce
1½ tbsp rice vinegar
2 tsp sugar
2 tsp cornstarch, blended to a smooth paste with a little water

Eggplant Stir-Fry with Hot & Sour Sauce

For the sauce, combine the soy sauce, vinegar, and sugar in a small bowl, stirring to dissolve the sugar. Mix in the cornstarch paste and stir until smooth.

Slice the eggplants in half lengthwise. With the flat side facing down, slice each half lengthwise into ½-inch/1-cm strips. Slice the wider strips lengthwise in half again, then cut all the strips crosswise into 1½-inch/4-cm pieces.

Heat a wok over high heat, then add 5 tablespoons of the oil. Add the eggplant and bell peppers and stir-fry for 2–3 minutes, until just beginning to color. Remove from the wok and drain on paper towels.

Heat the remaining tablespoon of oil in the wok over high heat. Stir-fry the water chestnuts, scallions, ginger, garlic, and chile for 1 minute.

Return the eggplant and bell pepper to the wok. Reduce the heat to medium and add the sauce and stock. Stir-fry for 2–3 minutes, until slightly thickened. Garnish with sesame seeds and scallions. Serve immediately.

SERVES 2

2 tsp peanut or corn oil
a few drops of sesame oil
1 small garlic clove, finely
    chopped
pinch of Chinese five-
    spice powder
1 carrot, diced

2 baby corn, halved and
    thinly sliced
2 tbsp water
small handful of baby
    spinach, tough stems
    removed, finely sliced
1¼ cups cold cooked
    brown or white rice

dash of soy sauce
1 tsp sesame seeds
    (optional)
small pat of unsalted
    butter
1 egg, beaten

Chinese Rice with Omelet Strips

Heat a wok over medium–high heat, then add the oils. Add the garlic, five-spice powder, carrot, and baby corn and stir-fry for 5 minutes, stirring and tossing continuously to prevent the spices and vegetables from burning and sticking.

Add the water and stir-fry for 2 minutes, then mix in the spinach and cook, stirring frequently, for an additional 2 minutes, or until the vegetables are tender.

Add the rice and soy sauce to the wok and heat through. Mix in the sesame seeds, if using.

Meanwhile, melt the butter in a small heavy-bottom skillet and add the egg. Swirl the egg until it covers the bottom of the skillet. Cook until the egg has set and is cooked through, then turn out onto a plate. Cut the omelet into strips or pieces.

Transfer the rice to individual serving bowls and arrange the omelet on top. Serve immediately.

SERVES 4-6

2 eggs
½ tsp salt
pinch of white pepper
small pat of butter
2 tbsp peanut or corn oil
1 tsp finely chopped
   garlic

1 small onion, finely sliced
1 green bell pepper,
   seeded and finely
   sliced
2¼ cups cold cooked
   rice
1 tbsp light soy sauce

1 tbsp finely chopped
   scallion
1 cup fresh bean sprouts
dash of sesame oil

Egg Fu Yung

Beat the eggs with the salt and pepper. Heat the butter in a small heavy-bottom skillet and add the beaten egg. Swirl the egg until it covers the bottom of the skillet. Cook until the egg has set and is cooked through, then turn out onto a plate. Cut the omelet into strips or pieces.

Heat a wok over medium–high heat, then add the peanut oil. Stir-fry the garlic until fragrant. Add the onion and stir-fry for 1 minute, then add the bell pepper and stir for an additional minute. Stir in the rice and, when the grains are separated, stir in the soy sauce and cook for 1 minute.

Add the scallion and omelet strips and stir well. Finally, add the bean sprouts and sesame oil and stir-fry for 1 minute. Serve immediately.

SERVES 4

2 tbsp peanut or corn oil
6 scallions, chopped
2 garlic cloves, chopped
2 fresh green chiles,
    seeded and chopped

2 zucchini, cut into thick
    slices
4 oz/115 g shiitake
    mushrooms, halved
½ cup fresh bean sprouts
½ cup cashew nuts,
    toasted

a few fresh garlic chives,
    snipped
4 tbsp Thai soy sauce
1 tsp Thai fish sauce
cooked rice noodles,
    to serve

Zucchini & Cashew Curry

Heat a wok over medium-high heat, then add the oil. Stir-fry the scallions, garlic, and chiles for 1–2 minutes, until softened but not browned.

Add the zucchini and mushrooms and cook for 2–3 minutes, until tender.

Add the bean sprouts, cashew nuts, garlic chives, soy sauce, and fish sauce and stir-fry for 1–2 minutes.

Serve immediately with rice noodles.

SERVES 4

10½ oz/300 g dried fine soba (buckwheat) noodles
3 tbsp peanut or corn oil
1 tsp dried ginger
1 tbsp rice vinegar
1½ tsp sesame oil
1 tsp light soy sauce

¾ cup fresh bean sprouts
¾ cup snow peas, thinly sliced
4 scallions, chopped
2 garlic cloves, crushed
1 red bell pepper, seeded and very thinly sliced

½ head of cabbage, thinly shredded
small handful of fresh cilantro leaves
pepper
toasted sesame seeds, to garnish

Wok-Fried Soba Noodles

Cook the noodles in a saucepan of boiling water for 3 minutes, or according to the package directions, until tender. Drain well, then add to a bowl of cold water and use your hand to swish around to remove all the starch. Drain again, then put into another bowl of cold water and set aside.

Put 2 tablespoons of the peanut oil into a large bowl and stir in the ginger. Beat in the vinegar, sesame oil, and soy sauce. Add pepper to taste.

Drain the noodles very well, shaking off any excess water, then add to the bowl. Add the bean sprouts, snow peas, scallions, garlic, bell pepper, and cabbage and use your hands to mix together. Season to taste with pepper. If you're not cooking immediately, cover the bowl with plastic wrap and chill in the refrigerator until 10 minutes before you want to cook.

Heat a wok over medium–high heat, then add the remaining peanut oil. Add the noodles and vegetables and stir-fry for 3–5 minutes, until all the vegetables are hot and just tender. Add the cilantro leaves and stir them through.

Transfer the noodles and vegetables to individual serving bowls and sprinkle with the sesame seeds. Serve immediately.

SERVES 2

1 lb/450 g mixed small mushrooms, such as cremini, enoki, and buna shimeji
6 tbsp peanut or corn oil
1 tsp crushed coriander seeds

1 fresh bay leaf
6 oz/175 g green beans
1 large garlic clove, thinly sliced
3 tbsp lemon juice
2 tsp soy sauce

2 tbsp chopped fresh cilantro
2 tsp sesame oil
2 tsp sesame seeds
salt and pepper

Mushrooms & Green Beans with Lemon & Cilantro

Wipe the mushrooms with damp paper towels. If using clumping mushrooms, such as enoki and buna shimeji, slice off the root and separate the clump. Slice any large mushrooms in half.

Heat a wok over medium–high heat, then add the peanut oil. Add the coriander seeds and bay leaf and fry for a few seconds to flavor the oil. Add the mushrooms and beans and stir-fry for 5 minutes.

Stir in the garlic, lemon juice, and soy sauce. Season to taste with salt and pepper and stir-fry for 2 minutes. Sprinkle with the cilantro, sesame oil, and sesame seeds and fry for a few seconds. Serve immediately.

SERVES 4

4 oz/115 g green beans
2 cups snow peas
1 carrot
8 asparagus spears
½ red bell pepper,
    seeded

½ orange bell pepper,
    seeded
½ yellow bell pepper,
    seeded
2 celery stalks
3 scallions
2 tbsp peanut or corn oil

1 tsp finely chopped fresh
    ginger
2 garlic cloves, finely
    chopped
1⅔ cups broccoli florets
salt

Summer Stir-Fry

Slice the green beans, snow peas, carrot, asparagus, bell peppers, celery, and scallions and reserve. Heat a wok over medium–high heat, then add half the oil. Add the ginger and garlic and stir-fry for a few seconds, then add the green beans and stir-fry for 2 minutes.

Add the snow peas, stir-fry for 1 minute, then add the broccoli florets, carrots, and asparagus and stir-fry for 2 minutes.

Add the remaining oil, the bell peppers, celery, and scallions and stir-fry for an additional 2–3 minutes, or until all the vegetables are just tender. Season to taste with salt and serve immediately.

SERVES 4

2 lb/900 g waxy potatoes
2 tbsp peanut or corn oil
1 yellow bell pepper,
   seeded and diced
1 red bell pepper, seeded
   and diced
1 carrot, cut into
   matchsticks

1 zucchini, cut into
   matchsticks
2 garlic cloves, crushed
1 fresh red chile, sliced
bunch of scallions,
   halved lengthwise
½ cup canned coconut
   milk

1 tsp chopped
   lemongrass
2 tsp lime juice
finely grated rind of 1 lime
1 tbsp chopped fresh
   cilantro, plus extra to
   garnish

Thai Potato Stir-Fry

Using a sharp knife, cut the potatoes into small cubes. Bring a large pan of water to a boil and cook the diced potatoes for 5 minutes. Drain thoroughly.

Heat a wok over high heat, then add the oil. Add the potatoes, bell peppers, carrot, zucchini, garlic, and chile to the wok and stir-fry for 2–3 minutes.

Stir in the scallions, coconut milk, lemongrass, and lime juice and stir-fry the mixture for an additional 5 minutes.

Add the lime rind and cilantro and stir-fry for 1 minute. Serve immediately, garnished with extra cilantro.

SERVES 4

3 tbsp peanut or corn oil
1 tbsp blanched
  almonds
1 large carrot, cut into
  thin strips
1 large turnip, cut into
  thin strips
1 onion, finely sliced

3 celery stalks, finely
  sliced
¾ cup Brussels sprouts,
  halved
¾ cup cauliflower florets
1 garlic clove, crushed
1 cup shredded white
  cabbage

2 tsp sesame seeds
1 tsp grated fresh ginger
½ tsp chili powder
1 tbsp chopped fresh
  cilantro
1 tbsp light soy sauce
salt and pepper

Winter Vegetable Stir-Fry

Heat a wok over medium–high heat, then add the oil. Stir-fry the almonds until lightly browned, then lift them out and drain on paper towels. Set aside.

Add all the vegetables, except the cabbage, and the garlic to the wok and stir-fry briskly for 3–4 minutes.

Add the cabbage, sesame seeds, ginger, and chili powder and cook, stirring, for 2 minutes.

Stir in the cilantro, soy sauce, and the reserved almonds and season to taste with salt and pepper. Serve immediately.

SERVES 4

3 tbsp peanut or corn oil
½ tsp ground turmeric
1–2 potatoes, cut into
 ½-inch/1-cm dice
3 shallots, finely chopped
1 bay leaf
½ tsp ground cumin

1 tsp finely grated fresh
 ginger
¼ tsp chili powder
4 tomatoes, coarsely
 chopped
6⅔ cups spinach leaves,
 coarsely chopped

1¼ cups fresh or frozen
 peas
1 tbsp lemon juice
salt and pepper
fresh cilantro leaves,
 to garnish
cooked rice, to serve

Spicy Potato & Spinach Stir-Fry

Heat a wok with a lid over medium–high heat, then add 2 tablespoons of the oil. Stir in the turmeric and a pinch of salt. Carefully add the potatoes, stirring continuously to coat in the turmeric. Stir-fry for 5 minutes, then remove from the wok and set aside.

Heat the remaining oil in the wok and stir-fry the shallots for 1–2 minutes. Mix in the bay leaf, cumin, ginger, and chili powder, then add the tomatoes and stir-fry for 2 minutes.

Add the spinach, mixing well to combine all the flavors. Cover and simmer for 2–3 minutes. Return the potatoes to the wok and add the peas and lemon juice. Cook for 5 minutes, or until the potatoes are tender.

Remove the wok from the heat and discard the bay leaf, then season to taste with salt and pepper. Garnish with cilantro leaves and serve immediately with rice.

SERVES 4

scant 2 cups long-grain
  rice
1 tsp ground turmeric
2 tbsp peanut or corn oil
1 zucchini, sliced
1 red bell pepper, seeded
  and sliced

1 green bell pepper,
  seeded and sliced
1 fresh green chile,
  seeded and finely
  chopped
1 carrot, coarsely grated
1 1/3 cups fresh bean
  sprouts

6 scallions, sliced
2 tbsp soy sauce
salt
fresh cilantro leaves,
  to garnish
lime wedges, to serve

Chinese Vegetable Rice

Place the rice and turmeric in a pan of lightly salted water and bring to a boil. Reduce the heat and let simmer until the rice is just tender. Drain the rice thoroughly and press out any excess water with a paper towel. Set aside until required.

Heat a wok over medium–high heat, then add the oil. Add the zucchini to the wok and stir-fry for about 2 minutes. Add the bell peppers and chile and stir-fry for 2–3 minutes.

Stir the cooked rice into the mixture in the wok, a little at a time, tossing well after each addition. Add the carrot, bean sprouts, and scallions to the wok and stir-fry for an additional 2 minutes.

Drizzle over the soy sauce and stir well. Transfer to individual serving bowls and scatter over the cilantro leaves. Serve immediately with lime wedges.